Lost *CINCINNATI* CONCERT VENUES

of the '50s and '60s

Lost CINCINNATI CONCERT VENUES
of the '50s and '60s

FROM THE SURF CLUB TO LUDLOW GARAGE

STEVEN ROSEN

FOREWORD BY JIM TARBELL

THE
History
PRESS

Published by The History Press
Charleston, SC
www.historypress.com

James Brown at a 1966 Cincinnati Gardens show. *Photograph by Stu Levy.*

First published 2022

ISBN 9781540251077

Library of Congress Control Number: 2021949178

To Mindy

CONTENTS

Foreword, Jim Tarbell   9
Preface   13
Acknowledgements   17

1. Northern Kentucky   21
2. Cincinnati Gardens   39
3. Surf Club   53
4. Downtown Cincinnati   65
5. Seven Cities   75
6. Neighborhoods and Beyond   89
7. Babe Baker's   101
8. I'm So Young   107
9. The Beatles in Cincinnati   109
10. Hyde Park–Mount Lookout Teen Center   123
11. Black Dome   133
12. Ludlow Garage   147
13. 1970 Cincinnati Summer Pop Festival   161

Selected Index   171
About the Author   175

FOREWORD

*S*teve Rosen was born in 1950, a great time for someone whose DNA features a thirst for popular music and a career in promoting the written word.

A devotee of the "Top 40" at an early age, the first song that really got his attention was Jimmy Dean's "Big Bad John." A friend departing for college lent Steve, then a Walnut Hills High School student, his R&B, blues and early rock albums, and he developed a fondness for Chuck Berry, Jimmy Reed, Muddy Waters and more.

And once the *Jelly Pudding* program on the FM station WEBN came along in 1967, he also became enthralled with the new, progressive album rock. He used to drive downtown after school to pick up library copies of albums by Bob Dylan and the Paul Butterfield Blues Band or go to a friend's house to hear the latest by the Yardbirds or the Who.

I know it was before his time, but I wish he could have seen Ronnie Hollyman—the Quiet Man—at the Key Club in Walnut Hills. It was so unique—a pub cellar that held about fourteen people, and Ronnie Hollyman was in this slightly elevated part of the room, playing his guitar and singing "Christopher Robin" and other kinds of English folk songs. His wife was serving Swedish meatballs, and we were sixteen years old, drinking Hudepohl; it was something else.

And there was Seven Cities Coffee House on Calhoun Street—sort of an early-day taste of bohemia. Every room was decorated as a different country. Danny Cox was a charter member of the group there and turned out to be a popular folk singer, as were some of the ladies from Grailville out in Loveland. We'd go to hear folk music and act like we knew what we were drinking when we had coffee. And there was dessert.

Walnut Hills High School was known for providing a great foundation for someone wanting to go on to higher learning. This Steve did by way of Indiana University (in 1968) and then finishing undergraduate studies at the University of Michigan.

Once Steve was of college age, he became an eager concertgoer, seeing acts at Cincinnati's Black Dome nightclub, such as the James Gang and Taj Mahal. He also became a record collector and the Indiana University campus representative for Columbia Records.

That's how Steve and I met. Mixing business with pleasure, he came to my Ludlow Garage to hobnob with NRBQ and the Flock, rock bands that were Columbia Records acts. (I once did a concert with NRBQ in Louisville at Iroquois Park, and it was too much fun doing it in their hometown. It was band leader Terry Adams's birthday, and all the wives and girlfriends conspired to make cream pies and, on a certain signal, came forward and smashed Terry in the face with the pies.)

About that time, Steve also delivered an audition tape to me from the avant-rock band Screaming Gypsy Bandits, who were from Bloomington, Indiana, the home of Indiana University. They were truly unique—an eye-opener for all of us. They were interested in Ludlow Garage because they had heard that Captain Beefheart and his Magic Band were coming, and they wanted, in the worst way, to open for them—and they did. The band became one of my favorites.

Steve saw as many Ludlow Garage shows as his out-of-town college schedule could afford. Beefheart's two appearances and the Incredible String Band were his favorites. And he remembers Alice Cooper's act of riding a wheelchair up in the girders, the support beams for the Ludlow Garage roof. To this day, I don't know how he got up there or down, but he was up there for sure.

After college and before going on to journalism school at Northwestern University for a master's degree, Steve had a job—his "best one ever"—as popular music stock supervisor at the Harvard University Coop Bookstore's record department. The money wasn't good, but it came with free tickets to concerts.

After Northwestern, one of Steve's first jobs was in Clearwater, Florida, where he was primarily a police reporter and wrote a weekly music column. He jokes that the column allowed him, between murders, to see the Rolling

Stones, Tom Petty, Patti Smith, Bruce Springsteen, Jackson Browne and Elvis Costello.

Returning to Cincinnati to work at the *Enquirer* in 1978, Steve quickly went to Arnold's Bar and Grill, having heard so much about it. That left quite an impression, and he quickly became a regular, whether for lunch, dinner or an after-work drink—or he'd visit the courtyard, where most of the music was played. Arnold's had an extraordinary repertoire of live music.

At the *Enquirer*, Steve reported on city neighborhoods for several years and then was a staff writer for its Sunday magazine, where he wrote a monthly entertainment column and covered such 1980s destinations as Cincinnati Folklife, the Jockey Club, the Sha Rah Lounge, Sudsy Malone's, Jazz Live from the Hyatt, Roosevelt Tavern and a prerenovation Memorial Hall, where he and I shared the Fairport Convention show. It was a great, great event. Leaving for the *Denver Post* in 1989, Steve covered numerous arts beats, won a National Music Journalism Award and several state journalism citations. He also interviewed many movie stars in person while serving as film critic.

After five years in Los Angeles, Steve and his wife, Mindy, returned to Cincinnati in 2007, and he increased his freelance writing for *CityBeat*, the *Enquirer*, *Cincinnati Magazine*, *Soapbox Cincinnati* and other publications. We became better acquainted as he wrote stories about my past music activities, such as bringing the Grateful Dead to the Hyde Park Teen Center, the fiftieth anniversary of the Ludlow Garage, presenting Ravi Shankar at the old St. Paul Church in Pendleton and staging the Midwest Mini Pop Festival at the Cincinnati Zoo. Those were four one-of-a-kind events, and he got to hear my recollections, especially the Dead at the Teen Center—people still can't believe it.

With this book, Steve shares with us Cincinnati's extremely unique program of post–World War II music through the 1960s and its concert venues. We are so fortunate for his record of our history.

—Jim Tarbell

Jim Tarbell was the proprietor of the original Ludlow Garage, as well as director of the Hyde Park–Mount Lookout Teen Center, before going on to own downtown's Arnold's Bar and Grill. He parlayed his civic activism into being on the Cincinnati City Council from 1998 to 2007, where he served as the city's vice-mayor from 2005 to 2007.

PREFACE

*L*et's start off with an advisory notice. This book does not include every "lost" Cincinnati live entertainment venue that existed during the timespan I cover: 1950 to 1970. That would result in a long list—a book of names.

Instead, I have mostly focused my chapters on notable defunct venues with compelling histories. Some are renowned today, like Cincinnati Gardens or the original Ludlow Garage; others are forgotten but important, like the Seven Cities Folk Club near the University of Cincinnati (UC) and Babe Baker's Jazz Corner in Avondale.

Occasionally, I have taken on either a larger focus in a chapter—such as the Northern Kentucky scene or downtown Cincinnati in the Swinging Sixties—or, paradoxically, a narrower one, like the 1970 Cincinnati Summer Pop Festival at Crosley Field. But within these chapters, I have tried to mention as many other places as I could that have some connection to the main subject. If there's something missing that you want to know more about, don't fret; I've already got a good start on a second volume.

I researched this book by jumping into the proverbial rabbit hole of digitized newspapers and magazines—the *Cincinnati Post* (which from 1958 to 1974 was formally known as *Cincinnati Post and Times-Star*), the *Cincinnati Enquirer*, the University of Cincinnati's *News Record*, the alternative/underground *Independent Eye, American Israelite* and others, both local and national. I also spent a lot of time on websites, blogs and Facebook groups dedicated to both local history and popular music. (I have tried to cite these sources in the body of this work when using their information.)

I had originally hoped to cast a wider net, but very quickly, COVID-19 interfered with those plans. I could not, for instance, spend time with the Cincinnati & Hamilton County Library's bound copies of old Cincinnati newspapers, nor could I meet in person those involved in the city's past live entertainment scene or search through their scrapbooks and photograph collections.

Thankfully, I could use the main library's drive-up window to pick up books and other material. I could also conduct phone and Zoom interviews. And despite the extreme pressures the pandemic put on everyone, the staff members at several libraries and other organizations helped when I had questions that required them to check a resource. Those who did their best to keep the world of "academic research" going during this time deserve our thanks.

Through all of this newspaper reading, I came to several conclusions about Cincinnati's live venues of the 1950s and 1960s. First, there were a lot of cool places with exciting live shows going on in this city. Looking back now, many seem historic. I suspect a lot of people at the time took them for granted or just didn't realize what was happening. These "lost" venues include places so small or that so appealed to specialized musical interests that the larger public might not have been aware of what was happening as it happened.

Controversial comedian Lenny Bruce performed at a nautical-themed club inside a Western Hills bowling alley. Aretha Franklin, early on, was at a small jazz club in Walnut Hills. The Grateful Dead played a Hyde Park teen center.

Other times, you can tell from the tumult that accompanied the coverage that everyone knew at the time what a big deal something was—like when the city's now-iconic Jim Tarbell (who graciously contributed this book's foreword) opened his countercultural Ludlow Garage venue for progressive rock acts in 1969.

Reviewing all that action now, I am humbled. It's like walking through the Rock & Roll Hall of Fame, only in Cincinnati rather than Cleveland. Really, it's a bit like walking through an art museum and seeing nothing but masterworks. (And because I'm only focusing on "lost," or defunct, venues, I'm barely mentioning longtime auditoriums or concert halls that are still in business, like Taft Theatre or Music Hall and its ballroom. They had plenty of shows with now-iconic entertainment figures, too.)

Fortunately, there were journalists who "got it" as it was happening and covered it smartly and even poignantly. I'm so indebted to the *Post*'s Dale

Album by Dale Stevens (*right*) and Jack Clements (*left*). *Photograph by Andy Balterman.*

Stevens and the *Enquirer*'s Jim Knippenberg, both now deceased. To me, they are great figures in Cincinnati's arts and entertainment journalism. They deserve statues.

Based on the sheer number of his bylines, I'm not sure Stevens ever slept. It is not uncommon to find several stories a day by him. For this book's purposes, I only followed his live entertainment coverage. But he also wrote about films, food, theater and more. He started with the *Post* in 1956 and was there until 1989, only interrupted by short stints at the *Detroit News* and the *Enquirer* and with public relations. He also had radio and television programs while he was a *Post* writer.

Stevens was, in a word, hip. As local comic Jack Clements said in the *Enquirer* obituary that was published when Stevens died in 1997, "The town is different because he was there." (Stevens and Clements, by the way, even put out a 1961 comedy album on the local Fraternity Records label called *The Weird and the Beard*. Stevens was the "Beard.")

Jim Knippenberg, who died at the age of sixty-three in 2009, shortly after retiring from a thirty-seven-year career at the *Enquirer*, was rightfully celebrated at the time of his passing as an irreverently witty columnist who wrote about social events and the people who attended them. So, it was a revelation to discover his earlier writings for the paper while researching.

A young Jim Knippenberg. *Courtesy of the* Cincinnati Enquirer.

During the late 1960s, as a writer for the *Enquirer*'s excellent teenager section, Knippenberg became an impassioned champion of the creative changes in youth music and a supporter of the emerging social network among baby boomer youths. For instance, he was at the Grateful Dead's 1968 show at the Hyde Park-Mount Lookout Teen Center and tried to describe to his readers the effect their transcendent psychedelic music had on him. (I quote his writings in this book's chapter on the teen center.) He also wasn't afraid to speak out against the city's censorious conservatives (of which there were many in the late 1960s). When city leaders banned the Doors from appearing at Music Hall in 1969 after the band's singer, Jim Morrison, was arrested in Miami for indecency during a show, he called them out: "This all reeks very strongly of cheap politics and should be loudly protested."

His strong voice—like Stevens's—makes his music writing a joy to read now.

ACKNOWLEDGEMENTS

I have sought to credit my sources in the text whenever I used them, whether they are a previous story, a book, a website, a Facebook group, et cetera.

But beyond these sources, there are people who provided me with their special help—be it their encouragement, personal recollections of Cincinnati's lost concert venues and their significant performances, photographs and images, research, feedback, insights on book publishing or editing skills.

I'm sorry if I've missed anyone; I tried to keep a running tally, but that got complicated as this project stretched on.

First and foremost, I'd like to thank my wife, Mindy. As I was doing my work at a desk in the living room during the pre-vaccination months of the pandemic, she tended to her very busy job from her workspace at the nearby dining room table. We had to carefully schedule our phone calls to avoid talking over each other.

Next, I want to thank my commissioning editor at The History Press, John Rodrigue, who understood that we were "cursed to be living through interesting times" as I worked on this but remained steadfast in his support and suggestions.

Tim VonderBrink read the individual chapters as they were finished and made careful suggestions. Later, Anita Buck did a very careful and thoughtful job of fact-checking, proofreading and editing most of this manuscript; Dave Caudill also did the same for three chapters.

Jim Tarbell offered me his colorful memories and his many contacts from not only his career as a visionary Cincinnati concert presenter but also the concert venues he loved to visit before getting involved with Hyde Park–Mount Lookout Teen Center and Ludlow Garage in the late 1960s. (I should also add that I was able to draw from stories about Tarbell's musical pursuits that I wrote previously for the *Cincinnati Enquirer*, *Cincinnati Magazine* and *Cincinnati CityBeat*.)

Beryl Love, the editor and vice-president of news at the *Cincinnati Enquirer*, granted me use of the paper's photographs, and Jeff Suess, the paper's librarian and expert writer on Cincinnati history, tirelessly searched for high-resolution photographs of the subjects I requested.

Stu Levy, now a retired physician in Portland, Oregon, looked through the meticulously archived photographs he took of Cincinnati's live music scene in the 1960s, when he was a University of Cincinnati student, and provided me with images.

Bill Soudrette, a collector of all sorts of fascinating ephemera related to Cincinnati's modern live music history, served as a consultant and also provided me with images of posters, handbills and more.

John Kiesewetter, who covers all things related to Cincinnati arts and media for WVXU and whom I worked for at the *Enquirer* (on the suburban news desk) when I was first hired there in 1978, helped me immensely with his contacts and photographs related to his *Enquirer* and VXU stories about the Beatles visiting Cincinnati in 1964 and 1966.

Jeff Meshel, Michael Blackman and William Spear helped me immensely with their knowledge of the music and cultural scene around the University of Cincinnati in the late 1960s and early 1970s—I hope to use more of their information some day.

Also super helpful were Andy Balterman, a retired librarian with formidable skills at searching for information through public records, and Stan Hertzman, who offered the knowledge and contacts he had accrued through his time as a music fan and musician who ran entertainment booking and artist management agencies in the 1960s.

I'd also like to thank: Roger Abramson, Terry Adams, Danny Adler, Terry Armor, Eugene Barnett, Larry Butler, Danny Caron, Tom Constanten, Danny Cox, Jim DeBrosse, Carl Edmondson, Max Elkus, Nancy Felson, John Fox, Katherine Gartrell, Nancy Goldhagen, Melvin Grier, Ken Hawkins, Glenda Hertzman, Russell Hoinke, Rose Huber, Matthew Knott Johnson, Pat Kelly, Steve Kemme, Peter Kolesar, Linda Kreindler, Lou Lausche, David Little, Randy McNutt, Mark Neeley, Hasker Nelson, Tracy Nelson,

ACKNOWLEDGEMENTS

Richard Von Nida, Brian O'Donnell, Beverly Olthaus, David Pomeranz, Brian Powers, Lindy Ranz, Ronald Rantz, Chris Richardson, Christopher Smith, Tim Swallow, Midge Sweet, Steve Tracy, William H. "Prez" Tyus, Ron Volz, Bill Westheimer, Carole Winters, Sandy Wolfson, Frank Wood Jr., Douglas Yeager and Maija Zummo.

1

NORTHERN KENTUCKY

I didn't want this chapter on northern Kentucky concert venues of the 1950s and 1960s to focus too much on the two famous casinos/ showrooms of the area: Southgate's Beverly Hills Country/Supper Club and Fort Wright's Lookout House. There is an ongoing cottage industry of books specifically about them, their decades of illegal gambling and mob influence, Beverly Hills' presentation of big-name entertainers and the clubs' precipitous declines in the 1950s and early 1960s as federal prosecutors cracked down on them. In recent years, there's even been a sensationalist twist on that subject—authors wondering if the horrific 1977 fire at Beverly Hills that killed 165 people could have been started by mobsters wanting to force out the new ownership trying to revive the club without the "help" of organized crime.

Instead, I wanted this chapter to be about the other colorful (if not always swanky) destinations in northern Kentucky. This area, especially Newport, had a reputation of being "wide open" for live entertainment. It had offbeat venues like Joe's Lake, south of Newport, where, in 1956, you could fish for one dollar, enjoy a free lunch (if you were a member) and see acts like local hero Rusty York (he had a national rock hit, "Sugaree," in 1959) or country/ bluegrass player Frank "Hylo" Brown. (The nickname refers to his vocal range.) Brown was raised in southwestern Ohio and originated "Lost to a Stranger," one of country's finest barroom laments.

Northern Kentucky was host to musical acts that reveled in their high-energy emotional explosiveness. In 1958, you could go to Cedar Bar, also

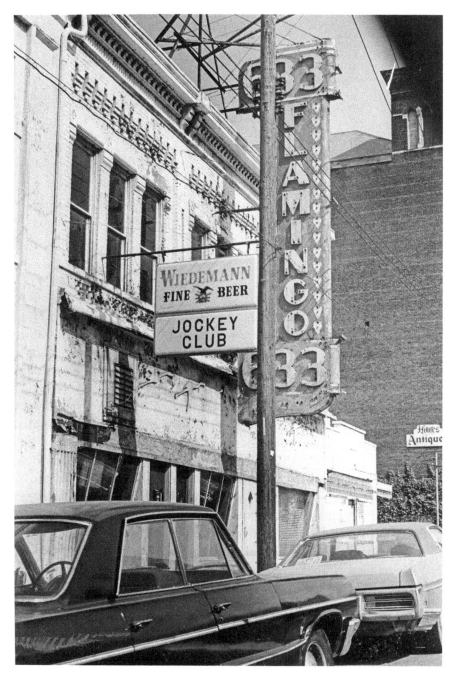

The Flamingo sign in 1980, when the club was empty. *Photograph by Dick Swaim; courtesy of the* Cincinnati Enquirer.

just south of Newport, to see the magnificently named "Mr. Rock 'n' Roll" Gene "Rubber Legs" Johnson and his Bony Maronie Band. (The band's name comes from a raucous 1957 rock hit, "Bony Maronie," by Larry Williams.) And there was Gooch's Web, the Covington club with perhaps the most unattractive motto I've ever come across: "A tangled-up mess; fall in."

I think I would rather have seen the entertainment at those unusual places than the typical acts that came through Beverly Hills in its heyday. (However, it would be hard to pass up a chance to see Little Richard doing a week of Mother's Day dinner shows at Beverly Hills in 1975, during its—and his—comeback years, with children accompanied by parents welcome at a reduced price.)

Northern Kentucky's clubs were super competitive, even daring, when it came to booking acts. They were willing to try many new acts and trends and were not uptight or prudish about it. In October 1959, Newport's Glen Rendezvous brought in singer/nightclub performer Christine Jorgensen—the transgender American woman whose sex reassignment surgery in Denmark had made international news. For Jorgensen's ten-day engagement, the club adopted a reservations-only policy in expectation of a high demand.

Amazingly, as the *Cincinnati Post*'s Dale Stevens pointed out, on opening night Jorgensen wasn't the only well-known transgender woman performing in the greater Cincinnati area at the same time. "And tonight, Tamara, who like Christine is a former GI turned female, opens at (downtown's) Cat and Fiddle," Stevens wrote. "Both of them can show you their war medals—including the Good Conduct Medal." (Tamara most likely was Tamara Reese. According to information posted at www.transcity.org, she was an army paratrooper and a Bronze Star recipient who medically transitioned in 1955. For a short period, Reese did a striptease act before ending it and withdrawing from show business.)

But the free-spirited entertainment did inexorably mix with the presence of vice—and that overlap needs to be covered here. This was especially true in the decades this book covers, when illegal gambling was still tolerated. And this led to some dangerous situations. Such a situation is illustrated in the story of how Charles Brown, the Rock & Roll Hall of Fame blues crooner and pianist, came to have a 1959–61 residency at Newport's Sportsman's Club. (I first wrote about this for the *Cincinnati Enquirer*.) While in Cincinnati, Brown recorded what has become a standard of contemporary holiday songs: the melancholy ballad "Please Come Home for Christmas." But Brown also, as he claimed in interviews before he died in 1999 at the age of seventy-six, may have been held there against his will by a kingpin of the region's illegal numbers racket, the late Frank "Screw" Andrews (Andriola).

Andrews ran several clubs along Newport's Central Avenue, near where the Licking River meets the Ohio River, that welcomed Black patrons and featured live entertainment, gambling and/or betting. The Sportsman's Club at 330 Central Avenue was the center of Andrews's numbers operation; he also had the Alibi Club at 310 Central Avenue and the Copa Club at 333 Central Avenue.

The Sportsman's Club had been in business since the 1940s, and Andrews acquired it after the owner was murdered in 1948, according to a paper prepared by Matthew DeMichele and Gary Potter of Eastern Kentucky University's Justice and Police Studies Program. This story was also mentioned in Robin Caraway's *Newport: The Sin Years*.

Brown had once been a star to Black audiences. From 1946 to 1952, first in a Los Angeles trio called Johnny Moore's Three Blazers and then as a soloist, the Texas-born Brown recorded such huge hits as "Merry Christmas Baby," "Drifting Blues," "More Than You Know," "Trouble Blues" and "Black Night." But after the hits and cash flow stopped, Brown needed money to bet on horses, according to Danny Caron, the musician who befriended him in the late 1980s and helped launch a "second act" return to popularity. "It was easy for Charles to get indebted," Caron said in an interview. "He could go through thousands of dollars a day. You gave Charles Brown a thousand dollars, and it was gone in an hour. He didn't have enough money ever to gamble. That makes it very easy for him to get indebted."

In an interview with me for the *Denver Post* in 1990, before he was set to open for Bonnie Raitt as part of his comeback, Brown recalled his Cincinnati/Newport days and how he got an employment offer from Andrews. "Mr. Screw was crazy about me. When he picked me up and wanted me to come there and stay and join the music department, he paid me $750 a week. Anybody I wanted to bring in, I could."

Brown became the club's house pianist. And one artist Brown brought to town to work with him was close friend Amos Milburn, another seemingly past-his-prime blues pianist and singer ("One Scotch, One Bourbon, One Beer" and "Chicken Shack Boogie").

Word of Brown's presence in town reached Syd Nathan of Cincinnati's King Records. In the 1990 interview, Brown recalled that Nathan asked him, "'Could you write something as good as 'Merry Christmas Baby?' I said, 'I don't know how good it will be, but I'll write.' He said, 'You and Amos go write one apiece and let me hear what you done.' When we brought it to Syd

The interior of the Sportsman's Club, 1961. *Photograph by Pete Peters; courtesy of the* Cincinnati Enquirer.

Nathan, he fell in love with mine." Milburn's "Christmas Comes but Once a Year" ended up as the B-side of Brown's King single.

"Please Come Home" opens with a memorable chiming bell sound. Philip Paul, who played drums on the record, said that the sound was produced by a gong played by Gene Redd, a King Records musician and an active performer at Cincinnati clubs. "I think that made the recording," Paul said. The song became Brown's first hit record in eight years and reached no. 21 on the *Billboard* Top Rhythm & Blues (R&B) Singles chart. Brown subsequently recorded other singles and even an album of Christmas songs for Nathan, but he never had another hit. While Brown claimed he wrote "Please Come Home" alone, the credits listed Redd as a cowriter.

Brown told *Living Blues* magazine in a 1994 interview that, in Cincinnati, he married an older White woman with children named Eva McGhee, who owned "one of the finest garages in Cincinnati." He characterized it as "a friendly marriage—it wasn't really love." Brown's 1999 obituary said he was twice divorced and left no family.

But he also told of wanting to leave town and being threatened by Andrews. He finally escaped, Brown recounted, when Internal Revenue Service (IRS) agents launched a devastating raid on Andrews's Sportsman's Club on August 22, 1961. The raid was part of President John Kennedy's crackdown under Attorney General Robert Kennedy (the president's brother), and it made headlines for days when it happened.

Fortunately for Brown, one "customer" may have helped him escape both Andrews and the federal bust. He was a Black undercover IRS agent who infiltrated the place before the raid. In his memoir *Three of the First*, Hilton Owens Sr. (who died in 2007) recalled, "I struck up an acquaintance with well-known ballad singer Charles Brown, who was famous almost everywhere except at the Sportsman's Club, where he was merely a fill-in during intermission for the main entertainer....Brown never discussed why he was trapped in the Sportsman's Club, and I did not pry." In his 1990 interview, Brown recounted those events. "That night we were playing there, this Black guy came and asked, 'Mr. Brown, would it take you and Amos long to get out of there?'"

Brown's path after that is unclear. Some accounts say he went to Los Angeles, but a 2004 CD collection called *The Very Best of Charles Brown: Original King Recordings* shows he recorded again for King on October 9, 1961, and off and on until 1968 while he was also recording elsewhere. A booklet that accompanies another CD says that Brown lived in Cincinnati in the late 1960s, too.

The late 1950s, '60s and '70s were years of struggle and obscurity for Brown before his return to prominence. His one towering accomplishment was "Please Come Home." The song becomes more appreciated with each passing holiday. When Bob Dylan played it on a Christmas episode of his *Theme Time Radio Hour* Sirius XM series, he explained, "I think it's actually against the law to do a Christmas program and not play one of his songs.... This is one of the best." Brown's extended stay at Sportsman's Club allowed him to create that song in Cincinnati.

Sportsman's Club had a convoluted history after Brown left. Andrews had sold the property in 1960, together with another club he owned called the Golden Lounge, to Newport's Municipal Housing Commission as subsidized housing. He set out to build a new Sportsman's Club at Second and York Streets. The *Enquirer* even got a tour in December 1961, with the uncredited reporter quoting from the charter of the International Association of Sportsman's Clubs, dated August 8, 1939, that had been posted at the door. It stated that the business was "devoted exclusively to the entertainment, education and fraternization of members of the Negro race all over America." The reporter's story further admired the way "the round bandstand and dancing area is offset by highly colored tapestries." The writer explained that sixty patrons on chairs could be accommodated at the sunken oval-shaped bar; overall, the venue could hold four hundred and also boasted a coffee shop and barbecue pit.

This new Sportsman's Club did open, but the big federal raid on the old one and the pending charges changed everything. Aside from the law, the club's creditors were also after Andrews. This continued off and on into 1966, when Andrews accused police of assault (it was dismissed, and he himself was fined ten dollars for interfering with officers of the law). The issue arose after he was accused of serving drinks past the permitted hours. At that time, it was stated, Andrews was merely in charge of maintaining the property for an uncle.

The Sportsman's Club remained open in fits and starts into 1968, and it booked notable acts as it sought a wider audience. A newspaper advertisement from June 1962 declared that "Frank J. Andrews invites everyone to the New Sportsman's Club." The feature act was the now-revered Cincinnati blues singer H-Bomb Ferguson and his orchestra, plus a floor show. In June, King Pharoh and his organ trio, with "famous singing group" the Egyptians, also performed.

In 1966, the *Post* reported that the club, which had been "open and closed with varying show policies since its construction," had hired a new producer/booker who was after top jazz and R&B acts. Some of the names mentioned were Lou Rawls, Cannonball Adderley, Junior Walker, Mary Wells and Martha & the Vandellas. It's not clear if they all made it there, but jazz organist Jimmy McGriff did play there, as did the Drifters and Jerry Butler (in 1967, with his first big hit in three years, "Mr. Dream Merchant").

In 1968, a *Post* advertisement promoted Leroy's Sportsman's Club, featuring the local R&B band Leroy and the Drivers, which had played at the club in the past and was labeled as "the big sound band." In 1985, the *Post* had a feature on Leroy Jones, who, by then, ran Hamilton County's top bail bond company and was a familiar courthouse figure. It recalled that he was singer for the Drivers and said he had learned his business skills by operating Cincinnati clubs, although Sportsman's wasn't named as one.

Andrews also was involved with the Copa Club, a nightery located at 333 Central Avenue. The Copa also had a history as a casino—you can find its gambling chips for sale at www.worthpoint.com. From 1959 to 1960,

Leroy and the Drivers with Tiger Lady, 1966. *Photograph by Stu Levy.*

it had an incredible run of the absolute cream of the crop of Black jazz, blues, and R&B music. During this period, the Copa was a one-thousand-seat nightclub with dancing. There is an excellent overview of its schedule at Cam Miller's website, www.queencityhistory.substack.com. "Andrews, with his 'connections,' was able to bring in some of the top Black musical acts of the day," Miller writes. "For the first 5 years of the club's existence, Andrews provided high-quality entertainment by booking mostly local and regional bands, as well as solo entertainers with the occasional national recording artist. But in 1959, with the help of the Cincinnati Jazz Club, he upped the ante with an amazing run of headliners."

The acts that were coming in, sometimes for several engagements during that two-year period, included trumpeter Miles Davis with his Jazz Kings (Cannonball Adderley on alto, John Coltrane on tenor, Winton Kelly on piano, Paul Chambers on bass and Jimmy Cobb on drums), B.B. King, Muddy Waters (with Brown and Milburn opening), the Platters, Cincinnati's own Isley Brothers, Sam Cooke, Fats Domino, Ray Charles, Count Basie, Brook Benton, Cab Calloway, Dinah Washington, Wilbert Harrison (whose "Kansas City" was a huge hit in 1959 and has since become a rock classic) and more.

But there was a certain risk for patrons when attending a venue linked to crime, no matter how colossal the talent of its performers. As *Billboard* reported in its December 14, 1959 issue:

> *The Copa Club, which continues to operate successfully with a policy of top jazz platter names on a four-days-a-week basis, narrowly missed a real blowout one morning last week when an anonymous phone caller directed the local gendarmes to the rear of the club, where they found eight sticks of dynamite stacked against the rear door. Fortunately the fuses had fizzled before hitting the explosives. The person making the phone call told Newport police that the dynamiters were out to get Frank 'Screw' Andrews, said to be one of the operators of the nitery.*

The Flamingo Club, located at 633 York Street, also had a gangster connection—but it's the club's possible connection to a pre-fame Jimi Hendrix that is most notable about its legacy today. It was a casino whose ownership once included the bookie Louis Levinson, later memorialized by

Newport's Copa Club in 1961. *Photograph by Pete Peters; courtesy of the* Cincinnati Enquirer.

having a hip Cincinnati riverfront bar and restaurant, Sleep Out Louie's, named after him. Incessantly pursued by law enforcement in the 1950s, the Flamingo's ownership still managed to survive, at one point presenting their venue in newspaper advertisements as a fancy restaurant like Beverly Hills.

There was an infamous 1962 incident at the Flamingo Club that, today, serves as a kind of bumbling, stumbling metaphor for the way illegal gambling finally ended in northern Kentucky and rock 'n' roll moved in to replace it.

In April, the press had turned up outside the Flamingo to watch former Cleveland Browns star George Ratterman, then the reformist sheriff of Campbell County (Newport's locale), stage a "raid" to seize club assets that would satisfy a delinquent tax assessment of $135.96. Also there, for some reason, was Andrews and a dog named Vegas. *Cincinnati Post* photographer Byron Schumaker naturally wanted to get a photograph of the goings-on. But there was a problem, as *Enquirer* reporter Margaret Josten explained to her readers:

> *A brown-and-white dog, owner and pedigree not known, stood inside the door, yapping at Mr. Schumaker. The photographer pushed the door slightly, attempting to aim his camera inside the Flamingo, where Mr. Ratterman and his deputies were conferring with the occupants. The door hit the dog accidentally, causing it to yelp in pain.*
>
> *At this, Mr. Andrews, reputed numbers racket king, rushed out the door at Mr. Schumaker, yelling about the dog. The photographer stepped backward on the sidewalk and Andrews struck him on the right temple, knocking him into a truck.*

Enquirer photographer Fred Straub captured the incident.

The night ended with Ratterman discovering that the tax bill had inadvertently been sent to a former (and deceased) owner of the club. Also, while all this was occurring, a Newport police officer came by and gave Ratterman's car a parking ticket. It took fifteen months, but Andrews finally faced trial on assault, and a jury deadlocked. "We felt the papers were trying the case and Mr. Andrews wasn't getting a fair shake," a juror said.

In retrospect, the most important thing that occurred at the Flamingo Club that day in April 1962 had nothing to do with the club's (and city's) sordid gambling past. It was about the future. During the brouhaha, one Charles Stagman invited the press inside. He had just arranged to lease the Flamingo and turn it into a "rock-'n-roll palace," in the *Enquirer*'s words. "I've got to overcome bad publicity," he complained. "This isn't fair to

Frank "Screw" Andrews slugs *Cincinnati Post* photographer Byron Schumaker outside of Newport's Flamingo Club. *Courtesy of the* Cincinnati Enquirer.

me. These people were here doing inventory on the property. They're not connected to me."

The era of Stagman's Flamingo Dance Club seems to have only lasted four years. But those were glory years if you love the music of boomer youth.

Stagman and his two sons—who bought the Flamingo outright in 1965—celebrated an already-older but not yet "oldies" side of rock 'n' roll. Flamingo Dance Club booked such exuberant early rock and R&B performers as Jerry Lee Lewis, Bo Diddley, Jimmy Reed, Hank Ballard, Tommy Tucker, Clyde McPhatter, Bill Haley and His Comets, Johnny Maestro and the Crests, Mickey & Sylvia, Chuck Berry and the naughty party band Doug Clark and the Hot Nuts. It also stayed true to the creators of dance crazes after their hits stopped, presenting Joey Dee & the Starliters ("Peppermint Twist"), Dee Dee Sharp ("Mashed Potato Time") and Gary U.S. Bonds ("Twistin' Matilda"). It let Chubby Checker headline in 1966, some three years removed from his big dance hits. It also promoted local acts like Lonnie Mack, Bo Dollar & the Coins, the Charmaines, and the Casinos. And it did occasionally get a buzzy new act—the Dixie Cups ("Chapel of Love" and "Iko Iko") did three New Year's Eve shows (the last starting at 3:30 a.m.) to usher in 1965; later that year, on-the-verge-of-stardom Paul Revere & the Raiders entertained. It also acknowledged the British Invasion with an early Beatles tribute band.

Looking back, one act really stands out, even among this superlative bunch. That wild singer Little Richard and his revue played three engagements at Flamingo Dance Club—on May 21 and 22, 1965; July 9 and 10, 1965; and May 27 and 28, 1966. There is reason to believe that a young Jimi Hendrix, using the name Maurice James, was one of the guitarists in Richard's band for those first two engagements.

Hendrix had played on other musicians' tours before—Steven Roby's and Brad Schreiber's 2010 *Becoming Jimi Hendrix* lists him as playing with the Isley Brothers both before and after his Little Richard stint, although their book doesn't list a Cincinnati appearance of him with them. But with vocal group the Tams, who had had a couple of hits, "What Kind of Fool (Do You Think I Am)" and "Untie Me," Hendrix appeared at a fabulous October 9, 1964 concert at Music Hall that featured such R&B stars as Solomon Burke, Jerry Butler, the Drifters, Patti Labelle & the Bluebelles and many others.

Hendrix started to get noticed for his innovative, stylized and downright revolutionary showmanship early. With Little Richard, Hendrix's talents seemed a match made in rock 'n' roll heaven. Little Richard hadn't had a hit single since 1958 and had spent a few years pursuing gospel music. But in early 1965, he put together a tour highlighting his 1950s rock hits. And in 1965, he recorded the wonderfully gritty, contemporary-sounding soulful ballad "I Don't Know What You Got (But It's Got Me)," with Hendrix on guitar. So, his U.S. tour caught a renewed, revitalized Richard, and he traversed the country with a touring band called the Crown Jewels or the Royal Family.

In a 2020 article for www.guitar.com, Michael Leonard investigated Hendrix's Little Richard roots and quoted comments that Henry Nash, the manager of Richard's touring band, made for Charles White's 2003 biography *The Life and Times of Little Richard*: "Jimi, to me, was never a precision guitarist. I know he was not a reading musician in those days, though he played well by ear. I regarded him as being innovative, creative and something of a stylist. He would sometimes play with his teeth and then put the guitar behind his neck and play with his fingers. This brought raves from the audience."

However, Richard wasn't completely enthused about Hendrix. He was an electrifying performer in his own right, wary of sharing attention. Britain's *Far Out Magazine* quotes Robert Penniman, Richard's brother and tour manager, as saying, "I fired Hendrix, who was using the name Maurice James all the time I knew him. He was a damn good guitar player, but the guy was never on time. He was always late for the bus and flirting with the girls and stuff like that." But it's hard to figure out when this occurred. The website www.earlyhendrix.com says Hendrix received payment from "Little Richard's Productions" for the sum of $166.55 for the period ending on May 27, 1965. (The payment statement turned up in an auction.) "I think it's pretty certain that Jimi played this (Flamingo in May) gig," said Nico Bauer from the website www.earlyhendrix.com, via an email reply to my query. "Of course, never 100% confirmed until there is a photo or a tape."

But there are also indications that Hendrix was still—or once again, if he had left in May—playing for Richard in July. *Becoming Jimi Hendrix* lists the July 1965 Flamingo dates as ones Hendrix played and then says that he quit Richard in mid-July. And in a 2016 Gay Chamber of Commerce newsletter article about a reunion of patrons of Fort Wright, Kentucky's Downstairs Club, a gay bar of the 1960s and 1970s, the writer says that "Little Richard and Jimmy Hendrix were known to sometime stop by when they were performing in Cincinnati." (Richard was gay.)

It seems the Flamingo Dance Club ceased booking and/or promoting its guest artists sometime in 1966. Bingo parlors had become a big and unofficially legal business—something like the marijuana trade in many states today—in Newport in the late 1960s, and the Flamingo Dance Club was part of the trend. (It made waves in the news in October 1966, when there was a dynamite explosion after Monday night bingo.) But in March 1968, the club was one of the five parlors raided by ninety FBI agents as part of a crackdown on bingo—the feds didn't view commercial bingo as so innocent.

What happened after that is outside of this book's timespan, but the venue did reemerge in 1982 as the punk rock paradise the Jockey Club, one of Greater Cincinnati's most important live music venues of that decade. It featured such acts as the Ramones, the Cramps, Black Flag, Husker Du, the Fall, Dead Kennedys and more. The club has since been demolished.

The Flamingo's major rival during the 1960s was Guys and Dolls on Alexandria Pike in Cold Spring, Kentucky, south of Newport. It was a bit out of the way but had a beautiful location next to a lake. Guys and Dolls (sometimes spelled in the press as Guys & Dolls or Guys 'N' Dolls) was owned by the late entrepreneur Ben Kraft. He previously operated a Southgate, Kentucky dance club called Black Orchid, but he sold it to buy Guys and Dolls in 1962. The name he chose was familiar to the culture at the time due to the popular Broadway musical and movie adaptation *Guys and Dolls*.

Teen and young adult dance clubs were big at the time in the greater Cincinnati area, especially in Kentucky, where bars could be open until later hours and casinos were being shut down. The scene was so big that the *Post*'s adventuresome Stevens took a tour of seven Cincinnati "dance spots in the rock-and-roll vein" in June 1963—Flamingo Club, Black Orchid, Peppermint Lounge, Hawaiian Gardens, Club Touchez, Club Tulu and Guys and Dolls. "I particularly enjoyed the Guys & Dolls Club, which has a smart décor and a reasonable professional program of continuous music," Stevens wrote. "Right now, owner Ben Kraft has corralled a semi-professional band of entertainers, including Carl Edmondson's house band, singers Gerry Diamond, J.T. Sears and Bill(y) Joe Royal, and current guest band Lonnie 'Memphis' Mack."

Through the 1960s, Guys and Dolls did bring in some big names, like 1962's New Year's Eve attraction and blues stalwart Jimmy Reed, early Motown star Mary Wells ("My Guy") and the dynamic singer Etta James. The club also hosted several of the "girl groups" who made some of the most distinctive music of the early 1960s—the Crystals ("Da Doo Ron Ron") and Ruby & the Romantics ("Our Day Will Come").

Guys and Dolls also created local stars, largely with the help of bandleader/ guitarist/singer Edmondson. The website www.buckeyebeat.com calls him "one of the fathers of Cincinnati rock-n-roll."

As a producer for Cincinnati's Fraternity Records, Edmondson put together two memorable national hits for local guitar hero Lonnie Mack: 1963's "Memphis" and "Wham!" Mack, in turn, played at the club (among others). Edmondson also wrote the teen ballad "Hey-Da-Da-Dow" for the

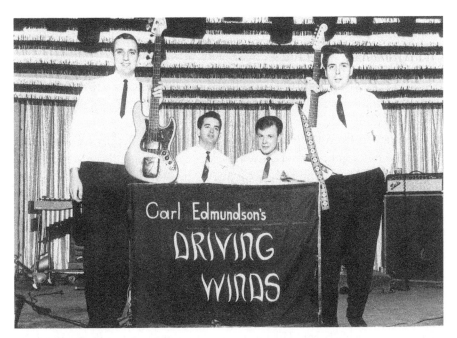

Carl Edmondson (name is spelled wrong in the photograph) with his Driving Winds. *Courtesy of Randy McNutt.*

male singers known as the Dolphins; he coproduced the recording, with Kenny Smith and Edmondson's band providing backup. It was a 1964 regional hit on the Fraternity label. And for two terrific local singers who went by the name 2 of Clubs, Patti Valentine and Edmondson's then-wife, Linda Parrish, he found the song "Heart," supervised the recording session and leased the result to Fraternity in 1966. It became the first of the duo's two formidable regional rock hits; the second was the equally strong "Walk Tall (Like a Man)." ("Heart" had been recorded earlier by Petula Clark; "Walk Tall" had been recorded by Verdelle Smith. Neither of the recordings was a hit.)

The young women of 2 of Clubs became major draws at Guys and Dolls when they were backed by Edmondson's band, the Driving Winds. "Ben Kraft, who owned Guys & Dolls, heard about me from people who'd seen me perform," Valentine told Mick Patrick from www.spectropop.com. "He came to listen to me, liked what he heard and hired me. At some point, it was discovered that Linda's voice and mine blended together really well, and we decided to become a duo. Linda was married to Carl Edmondson, who headed up the house band."

Edmondson and his Driving Winds had been playing Kraft's Black Orchid until they got extended engagements in Lexington, Kentucky, and Dayton, Ohio. "We were playing at the 77 Club in Dayton six nights a week, nine hours on Friday and Saturday," recalled Edmondson, now retired and living in Anderson Township. "Ben Kraft showed up there and said, 'I got a new club and I want you.'"

Edmondson liked the club's ambience. "It was basically all one room and had a fairly good-size stage and a dance floor, and all the way around were tables and everything," he explained. "It would seat about 400 people. Ben Kraft insisted on a band playing but then having a little space between songs for people to sit down. And people were dancers back then—they loved to dance. What made us special was we were basically White guys playing rhythm and blues. Our station wagon used to say 'a little shot of rhythm and blues.'"

Perhaps the biggest draw at Guys and Dolls was Billy Joe Royal, a gifted singer from Georgia who had a string of hard-driving country- and soul-tinged rock hits in the mid- to late 1960s; he played at the club regularly when he got his big break. His hits charted nationally but were major top 40 hits locally, especially 1965's "Down in the Boondocks," which still is played regularly on oldies stations. (Royal died in 2015.)

According to Edmondson, a keyboard player in his band known as Mitch Mitchell (his actual name was Bill Peters) knew Royal. He told Guys and Dolls owner Kraft about Royal, and Kraft arranged for him to come to Cincinnati to be a regular at his club. "Evidently, he paid him pretty well," Edmondson said. "Billy was quite an entertainer."

In Georgia, Royal worked in the studio with his friend Joe South, a songwriter and musician who had written the hit "Untie Me" for the Tams and later had his own smash records, including "Games People Play." When Royal returned to Cincinnati and Guys and Dolls after a holiday vacation in Georgia, he was excited with the result. "[He] said, 'Joe and I went to the studio and cut a song, and it looks like Columbia's going to pick it up,'" Edmondson recalled. "Halfway through the year, 'Down in the Boondocks' hits in this area—number one everywhere in the Midwest. So, Billy is drawing huge crowds at Guys and Dolls, and we'd also play Moonlite Gardens [at Coney Island] and LeSourdsville Lake [a defunct amusement park in Monroe, Ohio, near Middletown] with Billy Joe. The crowds were just incredible."

Royal's other hits (some penned by South) include "I Knew You When," "I Got to Be Somebody," "Heart's Desire," "Yo-Yo" and "Hush" (later covered in a psychedelic arrangement by Deep Purple). Royal became too big to stay in Cincinnati, but his occasional returns to Guys and Dolls were major events and Kraft went all out to promote them. For a show on December 11, 1965, Kraft purchased a huge advertisement in the *Post* featuring a large, wide photograph of Royal with a copy block in all capital letters, reading, in part: "Explosive singer who sky-rocketed to fame and appearances on *The Merv Griffin Show, Mike Douglas Show, Shindig, Hullaballoo, Where the Action Is* and *Upbeat* returns to his launch pad, Ben Kraft's Guys 'N' Dolls club tonite to entertain his original fans & boosters." And for a May 13, 1967 return, Kraft ran the same advertisement—but with a difference. It was more vertical in order to give co-billing (and a photograph) to 2 of Clubs. It boasted, "Greatest female singing act in the U.S." "The girls never hit the road," Edmondson said. "That's why their crowds were so big. They were drawing people from afar after they had their hits. They stayed at Guys and Dolls and kept packing them in." (Actually, 2 of Clubs did play at least one other locale; a 1966 *Enquirer* advertisement from a "genuine teen nite club" in Elsmere, Kentucky, called Granny's lists the duo as headliners.)

Early in 1966, business started to slow at Guys and Dolls, where the primary clientele was young. In a June 1966 interview, Kraft gave Stevens a startling and foreboding reason for this downturn. "[He] places the blame for the present lull in night life squarely on the war in Vietnam and the draft....And Ben is honest enough to predict it will stay bad for a long while," Stevens wrote. (If Kraft was referring to the war when he said "it," he was certainly proved right by history.)

Guys and Dolls did hold on, however, through the 1960s, even as Edmondson left and the hipper, newer clubs turned into venues for listening rather than dancing toward the end of the decade. In 1971, the *Enquirer* gave notice of a big night at Guys and Dolls, featuring four local bands at a benefit dance: the Ice, Apple Butter Band, Heather and Vision. In 1981, Bev Spoonamore bought the building, and it became a restaurant. The site now holds a Cracker Barrel.

In researching this story, I discovered that Kraft, at one time, built a patio by the lake for his patrons. When I asked Edmondson if his band had ever played outdoors there, he gave an answer that would bring a smile to any former member of a 1960s rock 'n' roll band or anyone who ever went to a club like Guys and Dolls: "They always said the band plays so loud, they didn't have to have outdoor shows."

2

CINCINNATI GARDENS

*W*hen the eleven-thousand-seat Cincinnati Gardens arena opened on February 22, 1949, it was primarily seen as a sports venue. Its very first night featured a National Hockey League team, the Montreal Canadiens, against one of its farm clubs, the Dallas Texans. That same year, Cincinnati got its own developmental team, the American Hockey League's Mohawks.

Over the decades, before the Cincinnati Gardens closed in 2016 and was demolished in 2018, it hosted a lot of sporting events and many home teams, but they did little to create a legacy. Cincinnati's National Basketball Association team, the Cincinnati Royals, had a surfeit of superstars but was never quite good enough to beat the champion Boston Celtics. The Royals left town in 1972, after fifteen years. And the parade of minor-league hockey teams that arrived after the Mohawks departed in 1957 is little remembered beyond the most die-hard of that sport's fans. There were also indoor football, soccer and roller derby teams that played there.

So, you can't really call the Cincinnati Gardens' sports history exceptional. But when it comes to live concerts, the Gardens consistently got major-league talent in the 1950s and 1960s, despite temperature and sound problems that consistently drew newspaper complaints. (The Gardens could expand capacity for concerts.) The greatest show of all, the Beatles' 1964 appearance, gets its own chapter in this book. But what follows here are some other highlights, with recent remembrances from those who attended these events, as well as excerpts from the newspaper coverage of the time.

The now-lost Cincinnati Gardens. *Photograph by John Kiesewetter.*

This is forgotten today, but Cincinnati Opera—lured by the possibility of higher attendance and more revenue—in 1951 tried hosting some of its summer operas at the then-new Gardens instead of its usual home, outdoors at the Cincinnati Zoo. According to Eldred A. Thierstein's *Cincinnati Opera: From the Zoo to Music Hall*, the opera opened at the Gardens ignominiously on June 26 with *Rosalinda*. It drew about three thousand fans—one thousand more than the zoo's pavilion could accommodate—but they didn't have a good time. "A number of problems made the first performance less than perfect. The amplification was not good, making everything sound too metallic. The floor started to sweat, caused by the hockey ice under the wooden floor put down for the audience, resulting in a very wet, stuffy atmosphere. Some actually walked through water."

The opera soldiered on with its scheduled productions of *Rosalinda* and *The Merry Widow* and even presented its add-on fifth week of *Aida* there, using little sound amplification. When that summer was over, the opera was through with the Gardens.

Before there were rock stars, there were cowboy stars. And singing cowboy Gene Autry was as big as they came. By the 1950s, a period during which Autry brought his traveling rodeo to Cincinnati Gardens several times, he was an established recording artist, had made ninety-three musical westerns and broadcast his *Melody Ranch* radio program and TV show on CBS. He was one of the biggest names in entertainment.

Autry's January 24, 1954 Cincinnati Gardens afternoon stop is well-remembered due to its documentation. A color poster from the event sold on Everything but the House in 2016; on it, a smiling Autry clutches his guitar near a photograph of horses Champion and Little Champ. It announces the "Hit Show of 1954," featuring, in addition to Autry and his horses, "Pat Buttram, Cass County Boys, Rufe Davis, Jemez Indians, Barbara Bardo, Carl Cotner, Melody Ranch Orchestra & Many Others." Another surviving poster shows Autry in white hat and fringed jacket, surrounded by American Natives. Also surviving from this show is a short *Cincinnati Post* article that reveals how much Autry was idolized by children. It details how nine-year-old Ray Larkins got to meet Autry courtesy of the *Post*'s Coca-Cola Big Wheels Club. "Ray had written the *Post*, asking for the chance to meet the singing cowboy," it begins. "Besides strengthening his determination to be a cowboy when he grows up, Ray had a ride on Autry's horse Champion and now totes a six-shooter given him by the Western star."

The 1950s really were a golden age for rock 'n' roll/R&B package shows. There were several crisscrossing the country at the time, and they filled with acts that, today, are honored in the Rock & Roll Hall of Fame. To have been able to see them when their now-classic songs were new would have been like being present for the creation of the world—if you love rock.

That's the way Stan Hertzman, who has had a long career in the music business as a guitarist, talent booker and manager, feels about it. He saw Buddy Holly & the Crickets twice at Cincinnati Gardens within a four-month span—at the January 23, 1958 *America's Great Teen-Age Recording Stars* show headlined by the Everly Brothers, and on April 14, at *Alan Freed's Big Beat* revue with Jerry Lee Lewis, the main attraction. (Holly had also come to the Gardens on September 11, 1957, with the *Biggest Show of Stars* caravan.) "Buddy Holly was the last act in the first half of [the] show," said Hertzman, who got good tickets through a friend. Because Holly and the Crickets were marketed separately by their record company, Hertzman didn't realize they played together live. "They came out, did 'That'll Be the Day' and 'Peggy Sue' and were so well-received they just totally upstaged everyone," he recalled. "People were standing on seats, going wild. He wound up doing 4–5 songs because he also did these Little Richard tunes. I was taken aback by this; I became a fan."

At the next show, Holly was followed by two impressive acts—Chuck Berry and Lewis. "But he stole the show," Hertzman said. "This was the most urgent, dedicated, serious musician I've ever seen in my life. Every note

A mind-bogglingly star-studded Cincinnati Gardens rock show in the 1950s. *Photograph by John Kiesewetter.*

meant something to this guy. He had rhythm; he could move to music in a hypnotic way. He had just improved so much from January to April."

Holly actually came to town for a third time that year on a promotional tour. Hertzman played hooky from the ninth grade with a mission in mind: he wanted to use his early-model tape recorder to conduct a phone interview with Holly. With help from a contact, he reached Holly at his hotel. "When he answered the phone and I asked, 'Is this Buddy Holly?' and he said, 'Yes,' I just about froze. I got 10 minutes of great conversation. He was a sweet man." Holly died in a plane crash on February 3, 1959, a tragedy immortalized in the song "American Pie" as "the day the music died."

If James Brown had a rival to the title "hardest working man in showbiz," it was Jackie Wilson, the Detroit-born Black performer who combined powerful singing with frenetic dance numbers and torch ballads with kinetic movements and a romantic appeal that had his female fans swooning and his male fans shouting him on.

The *Post*'s ever-busy entertainment writer/editor Dale Stevens attended Wilson's show with Jerry Lee Lewis, Ruth Brown, Bo Diddley and more at the Gardens on October 27, 1961, and he was suitably impressed: "Wilson, with his voice that suggests a legit tenor and his dancing gyrations, could, with the finesse that comes with time, reach the total audience," he begins. "As Jackie walked past me, towards the stage, completely disrupting the foolish disturbance Jerry Lee Lewis was wallowing in, he was mobbed by fans and soundly kissed by one gal several times. The girl then ran whooping back to her boyfriend." A bit further on, Stevens describes Wilson's stage presentation. "There was such general bedlam as Wilson took the stage that midway through his first number, a policeman walked on the stage and stopped the band. And the show, played under full house lights all the way to minimize customer antics, didn't resume until the crowd was reseated."

It's a little-known fact that the Beatles were not the first big British Invasion group to headline at Cincinnati Gardens. That "honor" fell to the Dave Clark Five (DC5), a lively but less artistically accomplished quintet that came here on June 4, 1964, already having had three top ten hits just since February—"Glad All Over," "Bits and Pieces" and "Do You Love Me." Their Cincinnati show was sponsored by WCPO Fun Radio, a rival to top 40 powerhouse WSAI, whose "Good Guys" were sponsoring the Beatles' upcoming August appearance.

The DC5 show was a disaster. As the *Post*'s Stevens reported, only two thousand fans showed up, and the promoters lost $3,000. But worse than the economic loss was the disastrous performance itself. "The stagehands

Gerry and the Pacemakers hold a press conference at Cincinnati Gardens, 1964. *Courtesy of Sandy Wolfson.*

seemed unable to make any of the six microphones work in any sensible combination, so the singing was erratic, announcements by Clark impossible, and it moved the friendly English boy to apologize to the crowd for 'the disgusting mikes [*sic*] in this place,'" Stevens wrote. The band played for no more than twenty minutes.

The aftermath became a big story in the newspaper's entertainment pages, with disappointed fans writing in and Stevens wondering if this was a bad omen for the Beatles' upcoming show. He also wondered if tense negotiations between the Gardens and the musicians' union might have played a role in the debacle. That drew a retort from the union's Eugene Frey, stating that his group had not asked the promoters to hire extra musicians and that a sister union had not "sabotaged" the show.

The success of the packed Beatles concert fueled a rush to bring top British Invasion acts to the Gardens. There were several subsequent shows. On Halloween in 1964, two Liverpool Merseybeat acts with close ties to the Beatles—Gerry and the Pacemakers ("Don't Let the Sun Catch You Crying" and "Ferry Cross the Mersey") and Billy J. Kramer & the Dakotas ("Bad to Me" and "Little Children")—came, along with local guitar hero Lonnie Mack ("Memphis") and the Angels ("My Boyfriend's Back").

In attendance were high school students Sandy Wolfson and Judy Schneider of North Avondale. Wolfson shared her memories:

> On the way to our seats, we ran into Dale Stevens, who wrote entertainment articles for the Cincinnati Post. I'd met him a few times before, a very nice man. After telling him we loved seeing all the British groups at the Gardens, he arranged for us to go backstage—where we stayed during the entire concert (but we were able to hear all the music)!
>
> We spent most of the time talking to Gerry's brother Freddie [who died in 2006; Gerry died in early 2021], the group's drummer. Freddie was very friendly but seemed quite homesick and showed us photos of his family from back in Liverpool. We had such a wonderful time chatting and getting autographs, and then we were allowed to attend the press conference as well. At the end of the concert, Freddie gave us a dollar bill for our bus fare. Neither Judy nor I can remember if or why we didn't have enough money. When we left the Gardens, we couldn't bear parting with the dollar, so we tore it in half so we could each have a memento. We both still have our halves after all these years!

As problematic as the Dave Clark Five show was, it was smooth sailing compared to Judy Garland's May 29, 1965 appearance at Cincinnati Gardens. The Garland concert made national news for all the wrong reasons. The best account of it was written up in 1983 as a colorful, empathetic remembrance by the *Post*'s Stevens. (He does say the show's top ticket price was $25.00 when his own reporting at the time pegged the top price as $7.50. Both seem like a bargain today to see a legendary performer of Garland's status.)

Stevens recounts how, as a six-song eighteen-minute first half was followed by an approximately hour-long intermission, local promoter Dino Santangelo called him into the dressing room. "Judy was sitting at her dressing table, just staring. She was surrounded by men I was told were her doctors. She was unable to continue the show, they told me. Santangelo had brought me there so I would understand this was not his fault." After Stevens returned to his front-row seat, he saw Garland come to the stage. "[She] was brought from the dressing room, glassy eyed, pale, not quite distraught, supported on each arm by a doctor. It was remarkable. She was there in front of the microphone, looking out into space but on exhibit, as much as to say, 'Look, I'm really sick.'"

The crowd, which Stevens had pegged at just three thousand while others reported it at four thousand, accepted her decision but were angry that there were no refunds. Legally, Stevens explained, half of a show was considered an official event. But after angry fans broke a ticket window, police asked Stevens to announce that refund information would be forthcoming at a later date. "To this day, I have friends who have saved their tickets as souvenirs of a bizarre happening and keep asking me when they can get their [money] back," he wrote in 1983. Garland died in 1969.

Because his label was Cincinnati's King Records and he often came here to record at the company's studio, James Brown had a large local base for his riveting live shows. Music historians generally say that Brown needed his 1965 top ten hit "Papa's Got a Brand New Bag" to reach beyond his Black supporters and draw White teenagers to his shows. But Cincinnati Gardens records indicate that he already was making inroads there years earlier. On October 4, 1963, his show came to the Gardens, promising such (White) teen idols in support as the Dovells, Steve Alaimo, Lou Christie and Johnny Tillotson. It also had plenty of popular Black acts of the day—Solomon Burke, Theola Kilgore, Little Johnny Taylor, the Olympics, the Crystals, Carla Thomas and Ted Taylor. But this was not promoted as a multi-act revue; it was advertised clearly as a James Brown show. (Stevens, in reviewing it, said some of those advertised acts were mediocre; others didn't show.)

Newspaper files show that Brown returned to the Gardens repeatedly in the 1960s (and also once to the historic Castle Farm venue with his *Prisoner of Love* show). He appeared twice in 1965, the year of his big commercial breakthrough. The second of those shows occurred on November 6—one day before another artist with a specialized following, folk/protest singer Bob Dylan, appeared at Music Hall on the tour that touted his own top 40 breakthrough, the rock 'n' roll classic "Like a Rolling Stone." He was doing half his show as an acoustic minstrel and half as a born-again rocker with support from the electrified band the Hawks (which later evolved into The Band.)

The *Post*'s perceptive Stevens used the occasion to write a compare-and-contrast review of both shows under the headline "James Brown and Bob Dylan: Unique."

Stevens loved Brown: "[He] is a mixture of every form of show business. He sings, every syllable is choreographed so that either he is dancing or the three Flames dance behind him, and he preaches love in the same way many preachers preach religion....It is pure emotion communicated with amazingly nervy technique."

And he had high regard for Dylan, who drew three thousand fans to Music Hall:

"He has a double uniqueness, since his poetic songs have made him as important in the folk field these days as were Leadbelly, Jimmie Rodgers and Woody Guthrie before him." But Stevens was not sold when Dylan, in his show's second half, plugged in. "The audience accepted both sides of Dylan, but as a rock-and-roller, his message is difficult to decipher. I'm wondering if this is an added dimension or merely half a Dylan."

The *Biggest Show of Stars* concert on November 12, 1965, used a title that harkened back to 1950s package shows, but it presented acts associated with Detroit's still-new Motown Records, which was reaching its apex in creating a new sound that would forever change music history. On this one amazing bill were the Four Tops, the Temptations, Martha and the Vandellas, Stevie Wonder, Jr. Walker and the All Stars, the Marvelettes, the Spinners, Kim Weston and more—all for $1.75 to $3.50 per ticket.

Next to the Beatles, the Rolling Stones were the biggest rock band to emerge from the British Invasion. (They still are as of the time of this writing.) So, it's a shock to discover that when they came to the Gardens on a Saturday night, November 12, during Thanksgiving weekend in 1965, only 2,500 turned out. (They had played in Dayton earlier that day, which could have cut into the crowd size.)

Glenda Hertzman, Stan's wife, remembers the show well. "I was a freshman in college then, and when I first got to school that fall, 'Get Off My Cloud' was really popular," she said.

> *My niece, who's my age, and I decided we would go at the last minute. We didn't have tickets ahead of time or anything. We drove from Middletown to Cincinnati in my parents' English Ford, an Anglia that was standard shift. We got not really good seats, but when we all realized there weren't many people there, we all started going down to better and better seats.*
>
> *I remember [Stones guitarist] Brian Jones because he had on red pants and a white turtleneck and sat cross-legged on stage playing guitar. And at one point, [Gardens staff or police] turned on the house lights because they said we were all being too rowdy. So, part of the show was*

The Rolling Stones on stage at the Cincinnati Gardens, 1965. *Photograph by Stu Levy.*

Getting to see Brian Jones, who died in 1969, was special for those who attended the Rolling Stones concert. *Photograph by Stu Levy.*

with the house lights up. I don't know why they thought we were being rowdy for the Stones. We weren't loud at all—just happy.

"They were wonderful," she said of the Stones. "It was so memorable, especially if you went to the [1964] Beatles concert, which was so crowded that you couldn't hear anything."

According to Stevens's *Post* review, the Rolling Stones played for about twenty-five minutes, and the highlights were their three then-recent hits— "Get Off My Cloud," "Satisfaction" and "The Last Time." He referred to them as "good rocky, building bluesy tunes." And he criticized the police for being too rough with the "enthusiastic kids." Stevens also praised opening act the Vibrations, an R&B group that had cut the first version of "Hang on Sloopy" under the title "My Girl Sloopy."

Stan Hertzman said that the poor attendance of this show was the reason the Rolling Stones didn't return to Cincinnati until 1989, when they played Riverfront Coliseum. "They hated Cincinnati," he said. "They thought it was just awful. That's why we never saw a tour date by them until the 1980s."

It's a mistake to dismiss the Monkees as a passing fad and "kids' stuff" of no lasting value, as so many adults and older teenagers did during the brief stint when the quartet ruled television with a hybrid music/sitcom show and the top 40 with hits like "I'm a Believer" and "Daydream Believer." The rap was they were an artificial Beatles group with little musical value. But the group was still touring and still making new music deep into the 2010s, even after the death of singer Davy Jones in 2012. And after bassist/keyboardist Peter Tork died in 2019, singer/drummer Micky Dolenz and guitarist/singer Mike Nesmith planned a 2020 tour. The COVID-19 pandemic postponed it.

When the young, super-hot group announced plans for a New Year's Eve show at the Gardens in 1966, *Post* writer Hap O'Daniel opined that they might not do well. "One wonders how the Monkees will do in person, especially in view of the date," he wondered. "They really aren't a musical act as such but a TV situation comedy team. Now, if you really want a musical act, how about Thelonious Monk and the Monkees?" But he went to the show (which was at 4:00 p.m.) and seemed distracted by the intense crowd noise and picture-taking. But he did provide a concert description, reporting that the band drew eight thousand fans and the show grossed $35,000.

When the Monkees returned on July 28, 1967, with opening act the Sundowners (the New York band had replaced the wildly inappropriate original opener, Jimi Hendrix, after he started seven shows and departed),

Hey, hey, they're the Monkees at Cincinnati Gardens. *Photograph by Stu Levy.*

O'Daniel tried them out again. He had been admonished by fans after his earlier coverage, so he was prepared. The result was a review that's still quite funny, if sometimes sarcastic, today. "It would not be possible to list all the songs they sang, because few of them could be heard," he said. "Musically, the Monkees were superb, as everybody knows. Davy Jones's tambourine, which set off peals of screams whenever held aloft, was played with a style never before equaled." He continued in that vein, also reporting that the group drew a crowd of 10,300.

By the way, there's still a demand to hear what the Monkees sounded like then; a four-disc *Summer '67: The Complete U.S. Concert Recordings* was released in 2001, but it doesn't include the Cincinnati show. And there's also a 732-page book titled *The Monkees: The Day-by-Day Story* from Andrew Sandoval and released in 2021. A passing fad indeed.

When Aretha Franklin came to the Gardens on July 14, 1968, she was at the zenith of her fame—in the middle of that fabulous streak of soul hits that began in 1967 with "I Never Loved a Man (The Way I Love You)" and continued through 1968 with "Respect," "Baby I Love You," "A Natural Woman," "Chain of Fools," "(Sweet Sweet Baby) Since You've Been Gone," "Think" and "The House that Jack Built"/"I Say a Little Prayer." It appears she had last been in Cincinnati in 1964, when she was trying to establish herself as a jazz/pop stylist with an appearance at the annual Ohio Valley Jazz Festival. Consequently, it was no surprise when the *Post* reported she would be getting the top price ever paid to see a solo female vocalist for a one-night stand in Cincinnati.

Reporting on the show, the *Enquirer*'s James Wilber said that "Miss Franklin was an absolute hit with her multitudinous following and succeeded in attracting one of the larger concert crowds at the Gardens this year." He cited an attendance of eight thousand.

Franklin was backed by the Aretha Franklin Orchestra under the direction of Donald Town and a female trio who provided vocal accompaniment. Aside from her hits, Franklin also performed such songs from her catalogue as "Come Back Baby," "Soul Serenade," "Night Life," "Don't let Me Lose this Dream," and a revved-up version of "(I Can't Get No) Satisfaction."

How much did live rock music change between 1964 and 1968? You can sense the seismic shift—from a fun way for young teens to let off steam to a veritable new religion for its growing number of adherents—when comparing the reporting on the Beatles' 1964 Gardens show to that devoted to the Jimi Hendrix Experience's November 15, 1968 show there. It was Hendrix's second Cincinnati appearance that year; he had done two shows at Xavier University's Schmidt Fieldhouse on March 28. But rather than exhaust the market, he was merely keeping up with demand. He had just released his *Electric Ladyland* album; what was probably his greatest single recording, "All Along the Watchtower," had recently been a hit.

The *Enquirer*'s Jim Knippenberg was at the November 15 show to cover it. He was a true believer:

> *The hyper-excited crowd welcomed* [Hendrix] *with deafening roars, piercing whistles and maddening shrieks. Hendrix was greeted as a guru of sorts.*
>
> *Jimi Hendrix really is the "heaviest" of them all. His show is so electric, so physical and alive that you can actually feel it in your blood. Once you see it, your mind will never be the same.*
>
> *In the course of the show, the scream of electric feedback, the sight of Hendrix picking the guitar with his teeth and his amazing acrobatics become common. With his guitar, Hendrix does everything but sell tickets.*

3

SURF CLUB

*O*n October 16, 1961, the *Cincinnati Post*'s Dale Stevens was speculating on the effect the closure of northern Kentucky's famous Beverly Hills Supper Club, which was planning to end its entertainment policy, would have on the city's nightlife. For decades, the Las Vegas–like nightspot had relied on locally tolerated illegal gambling to survive, and its showroom had brought some of the nation's biggest stars to town. But the law enforcement crackdown had finally come, and the nightclub was then firing its orchestra, its house trio and its pianist.

"Certainly, Cincinnati never again will have a big floor show such as Beverly provided," Stevens opined. "What is needed and likely would do business is a 300-seat room using [national] singers and comics." He even mentioned two possibilities—a downtown Cincinnati lounge called the Piano Room, which was then in the process of becoming a jazz club called the Living Room, and an entertainment spot in a bowling alley on the city's far west side known, incongruously, as the Surf Club. Otherwise, Stevens speculated, all the other clubs with live music would book only local acts.

Stevens was definitely right about the two clubs he named—they spearheaded a renaissance in big-name Cincinnati nightlife during the early 1960s. (The Living Room is featured in the next chapter.) But he underestimated the ambitions of some of the other venue owners to feature more than local talent. During the 1960s, especially in the first half of the decade, Cincinnati was alive with clubs presenting the elegant allure of fine dining, mixed drinks and top names in jazz, popular music, comedy and variety. But it didn't last, and it wasn't easy to survive while it lasted. Looking through old newspaper stories, you can find club owners repeatedly complaining about the rising cost of talent and the reluctance of Cincinnati audiences to pay cover charges.

The Surf Club should be celebrated, if only for one engagement that towers amid the club's other high points of entertainment. In July 1962, it booked a five-day engagement by the most controversial comedian of the time—and maybe ever. Lenny Bruce's often-profane, antiestablishment, satirical "sick" humor—he seemed to free associate through such subjects as sex, politics and American hypocrisy—had already gotten him arrested for obscenity in San Francisco. And his drug use had gotten him busted in Philadelphia. More arrests were to come in Philadelphia and New York, and as his drug use increased, it became harder for him to work. Bruce died of a heroin overdose on August 3, 1966, at the age of forty.

Bruce would seem way too dangerous for a Cincinnati nightclub—and one on the family-oriented, insular west side, especially. But Cincinnati did have an eccentrically formatted radio station: Newport, Kentucky's WNOP-AM, which played comedy and jazz records and possessed a certain beatnik-like savvy. At least one other station, WZIP, also featured some jazz programming. And Dale Stevens was a strong, popular journalistic voice in the city who also hosted a jazz radio show. As early as 1959, he had written a column in praise of Bruce's style of "new thing" humor.

On July 11, the day after Bruce opened, Stevens published an eloquent, understanding review of the show:

> *Lenny Bruce is both profane and profound. And if that seems a strange combination for a comedian, then don't call him a comic. Call him an orator, or even a preacher. A doctor, maybe.*
>
> *No subject is protected from his probing mind. There are almost no words he won't use. He delights in proving the sociological semantics of some rather rough expressions.*
>
> *Along the way, Lenny offends some of his customers. A few walk out. Many sit in semi-shock, moved occasionally to sudden hysteri-laughs based on incredulity.*
>
> *Bruce discussed his recent arrests on charges of using narcotic medicine without a prescription (that was thrown out of court) and using obscenity in his act (the jury found him not guilty on that one).*

Terry Armor, a longtime Cincinnati photographer who worked at the *Enquirer*, became interested in jazz and comedy after discovering WNOP, so he was at one of Bruce's Surf Club shows. He vividly remembers the comedian's unusual—some might say distasteful—approach to shaking his audience up with some pranks.

"So, he's up on stage, and he asks if anyone would have a piece of paper or a tissue," Armor said. "Somebody from the audience brings one up, and he lays a hocker in it, then folds it up and says, 'Now, I'm going to put this on the piano, and he'll think it's a request and open it up when he gets back from break.'" (The pianist didn't fall for it, Armor said.) "With Lenny Bruce, every place he went, the feds were after him. Toward the end of the show, he said, 'I want all the house lights down because I know the FBI is watching.' And then after it was dark, he said, 'Now, I'm going to piss on you.'"

The opening of the Western Bowl at 6383 Glenway Avenue was announced in 1958 and occurred in 1959. It was the project of George Panuska, John Brune and Robert Harpenau. The latter two were developers who were also building a nearby one-thousand-home subdivision called Green Acres. By 1960, the owners were already expanding the bowl with sixteen new lanes to bring the total to forty-eight; a large cocktail lounge with dance floor and orchestra stand; a meeting room; and parking for 550 cars. Once the work was finished, the partners hired Erwin "Erv" J. Hoinke Jr., an accomplished bowler who, with his dad, owned Hoinke Lanes in Price Hill, to operate the Surf Club.

The Surf Club had an early and valuable fan in Stevens. On January 27, 1961, he was already writing about a proposed comedy format at "our town's most beautiful nightclub." On February 3, the paper's "Gourmet Guide" weighed in: "Western Bowl is a place to eat—fine food," singling out its Mustang Room and "ultra-new" Surf Club.

"It had a bunch of big sharks and swordfish on the walls that these gentleman [the owners] caught and stuffed," said Russell Hoinke, Erwin Jr.'s son. "Why they chose a surf motif I don't know, other than they were big fishermen and had homes in Florida."

The *Cincinnati Enquirer*'s Arthur Darack, who wrote a column called "Off Beat," described his impressions upon seeing the Modern Jazz Disciples there in 1961:

> *The Surf Club sports a fish mounted gaily on the base of the wall, churning a spray of string and white gobs on near-cotton. An overhead net keeps out the flying fish. The jazz show keeps in the young, impressionable chicks and*

their escorts. The Surf Club is sprawling, plus, versatile, a haven for the bowler and the man who wants to be entertained in style, to eat in caloric confidence and listen in aesthetic bliss. It is quite a combination sandwich.

Until it closed as a club on September 20, 1963, and became a billiard parlor, the Surf Club displayed great eclecticism in its bookings. Aside from featuring local musicians, such as local jazz favorites the Dee Felice Trio, it brought in older, seasoned jazz and other acts—people like R&B saxophonist (and King Records star) Earl Bostic, trombonist Jack Teagarden, singer Sarah Vaughan, trumpeter Jonah Jones, comedian Henny Youngman, 1950s crooning sensation Julius La Rosa, old-school singer/bandleader Ted Lewis (whose trademark shouts of "Is everybody happy?" had galvanized the nation decades previously) and singer/orchestra leader Tony Pastor, who had heard Rosemary and Betty Clooney when they were singers for Cincinnati's WLW radio and hired them.

One such "old pro" who played the Surf Club was Jack E. Leonard, an aggressive insult comedian who got a head start on Don Rickles. He was also a big man who could be a magnet for trouble. One newspaper story tells of Leonard attacking a three-hundred-pound heckler; another recounts his anger when someone set off a cherry bomb during his set, scaring the audience.

The Surf Club also had a taste for bawdy female comedians like Belle Barth and Rusty Warren (whose trademark was a song called "Bust Your Boobies"). In a November 8, 1962 *Cincinnati Enquirer* story headlined "Rusty Warren Abreast of Times," which was apparently a positive review, E.B. Radcliffe wrote, "Being far from memorable, I find Rusty's unsophisticated chatter and piano patter about sex is right out of yesterday's burlesque. Only she doesn't work with the seltzer bottle or bladder bag belt over the head of a second banana, she does a boudoir chic sale."

Besides presenting all this mature talent, the Surf Club was hip to the fact early that baby boomers wanted relevancy and new ideas as they reached adolescence. This was a time when the Beats challenged conventional tastes, the civil rights movement grew and the youthful President Kennedy presided over an American Camelot.

Bruce represented relevance and new ideas, but so did the comedian who appeared soon after him: Dick Gregory. A Black man who drew his material from current events, especially the struggle for racial justice, Gregory had developed a penetrating wit and knew how to skewer American hypocrisy. One of his famous lines was, "In the South, White folks don't care how close you live to them as long as you don't get too big. Up north, they don't care how big you get, as long as you don't live too close."

In the early 1960s, Gregory was coming into demand at clubs that appealed to White audiences. Gregory first came to the Surf Club—and Cincinnati—for a stint between March 14 and March 16, 1961, just as he was starting to draw national publicity and standing-room-only crowds. For his July 1962 return, Stevens noted, Gregory was getting $5,000; he was already being offered $10,000 per week elsewhere. Further, he had received a $25,000 advance for a book. Gregory had also been the main attraction in a touring production of Black artistry called *Larry Steele's Smart Affairs of 1962*, which had just played Dayton's Memorial Hall in February.

In an interview during his 1962 appearance, Stevens asked Gregory if he was surprised by his bookings at such "White" clubs. "There are two reasons [for it]," Gregory answered. "You'd be surprised how many club owners don't know there ARE Negro comics. And a lot of agents just assume a club won't hire a Negro and don't offer them a room." Stevens also asked Gregory if he was looking forward to becoming a millionaire. His reply was, Stevens reported, "'Oh, yeah.' And he didn't even chuckle. You have to figure he meant it."

Actually, this interview is a rare case of Stevens getting it wrong. He viewed Gregory as someone finding and enjoying wealth and acceptance within the mainstream entertainment business. But the 1960s had other plans for him. Gregory went to Selma, Alabama, in 1963 to work in the civil rights movement. He also went to Philadelphia, Mississippi, in 1964 to hunt for the bodies of murdered civil rights activists. He then dedicated his life to protests, hunger strikes and arrests in opposition to racism and the Vietnam War, while also building a dietary food business. He died in 2017 and was the subject of a Showtime documentary, *The One and Only Dick Gregory*, in 2021.

By the time Phyllis Diller made her first Surf Club appearance at the end of May 1962, she already had a devoted local audience. More than a year earlier, she had played Dayton's chic Racquet Club, and forty Cincinnati women had rented a Greyhound bus to go see her. Diller's Surf Club stint was so popular that she had to add shows. The *Post*'s Stevens had to stand to review her show, which didn't deter him from writing a rave review that also showed some interesting insight (for 1962) into how Diller toyed with gender stereotypes.

What's her secret? It's a montage of her many vitals. Nobody tops her for sheer professionalism. Her ability to pitch her quick one-liners without wasting a word is priceless....With Phyllis Diller, all the necessary ingredients are there—the wild clothes, the wilder hair, the witch-like face and an indeterminate figure. No woman watching Phyllis has to worry what her husband is thinking. Phyllis looks funny, and she is funny. She is sexless, deliberately, and what other comedienne has ever been so pleasing to other women....Phyllis Diller is America's funniest woman. More important, she might be its brightest as well.

In 1963, when Diller was booked into Coney Island's Moonlite Gardens—a curious choice for a comedian, given it was an outdoor pavilion in a noisy amusement park—Stevens was undeterred. "I would go to see Phyllis if I had to stand in Fountain Square while she yelled from atop Carew Tower," he said.

The Smothers Brothers made their Cincinnati debut on September 25–30, 1962, a good five years before their landmark *Smothers Brothers Comedy Hour* debuted on television. With its mix of folk, comedy, rock 'n' roll and liberal anti–Vietnam War politics, the show captured the imagination of younger fans everywhere.

When the duo arrived at the Surf Club, Stevens saw them as one in a new trend of "folk humor" groups. But he also saw something more that would help them stick around.

Folk songs have become the peg on which the new school of performers hangs their comedy hats. But the main ingredients are sophistication and intellectuality. Were the boys just clowns using folk tunes, they would be a good act. Their important plus, the one that grows on you, is that they are musically valid. Their harmonic integrity on "Down in the Valley" is accomplished and stimulating. And the second voice part is intricate enough to keep you listening.

If Stevens seemed to be careful of not dismissing their musical chops in favor of highlighting their comedy, it's because he learned his lesson while reviewing Peter, Paul and Mary, who had made their area debut at the Surf Club a couple of weeks earlier, playing September 4 through a matinee on September 9. Their first big-hit record, "If I Had a Hammer" (The Hammer Song), had just been released and was already getting airplay.

In his review the next day, Stevens praised the act but saw the trio as primarily a "comedy team." Three days later, he came back with a mea culpa feature and, in the process of recognizing the group's personal commitment to its folk music, also noted the times were a-changin', to paraphrase the title of Bob Dylan's 1964 song. Peter, Paul and Mary would help popularize that and other Dylan songs, beginning with the hit "Blowin' in the Wind" in 1963. "I made the mistake this week, in reviewing their excellent act at the Surf, of thinking they were just an act and nothing more, entertainers more than folk singers," he wrote. "The reverse is true. The key thing about PP&M is that they are not a gang of college kids who drifted together to entertain at a campus party. They were conceived by Al Grossman, who discovered Odetta and Joan Baez and produced two national folk festivals at Newport, RI." (Stevens possibly didn't know it yet, but Grossman was also managing Bob Dylan, who at that time, was still a new folk singer.)

Amid all the cool, younger and sophisticated acts coming into Surf Club, it might be surprising that one of its biggest successes was the "cornpone" country act of Homer and Jethro. They did record-setting business playing April 3–8, 1962, including a *Jazz on a Sunday Afternoon* show, and they were rebooked for a later engagement. But actually, Homer and Jethro weren't what they seemed on stage. Henry D. "Homer" Haynes (guitarist) and Kenneth C. "Jethro" Burns (mandolinist) were consummate musicians and razor-sharp musical satirists, even if their "hick" aura hasn't weathered so well. Early in their career, they performed on WLW's *Midwestern Hayride*, and they first recorded for Cincinnati's King Records before moving to RCA.

"Funniest part of [the success] was the reaction from Homer and Jethro, who do not consider themselves hillbilly artists," Stevens wrote. "They were loaded for bear when they found out they were going to work the *Jazz on a Sunday Afternoon* program. Their specialty is 'Lullaby of Birdland,' which they do as 'Lullaby of a Bird Dog.' Not only that, they insist that the jazz audience is their best audience because jazz fans get all the sharp bits of satire the boys do."

The success of the Surf Club did not go unnoticed by other Cincinnati club owners. In response, some started to upgrade their Ohio venues and plan new showrooms and clubs. This was in addition to smaller jazz rooms around town, as well as the behemoth Castle Farm on Summit Road, near Roselawn, which had been open for

This unidentified female vocalist appeared at the influential Surf Club. *Courtesy of Jan Cella.*

almost forty years and was still booking a potpourri of acts. The then-new and nova-hot Jewish comedian Jackie Mason came to Castle Farm in 1962 to do a show sponsored by Adath Israel Congregation before he played the Surf Club. The Farm also hosted big bands, James Brown and even the occasional "teenage dance party," as it did on March 31, 1959, when presenting Link Wray, who is now considered one of rock's greatest guitarists, the Bell Notes ("I've Had It"), the Kalin Twins ("When"), Jesse Lee Turner ("The Little Space Girl") and, finally, Bill Parsons and the All American Boys Band. The last act presumably played the huge hit "All American Boy," even though the song actually was recorded by future Country Music Hall of Famer Bobby Bare for Cincinnati's Fraternity Records. The label inadvertently credited it to Parsons.

Built in 1924 as a "dining and dancing rendezvous with accommodations for 1,200," Castle Farm was rebuilt for $300,000 and reopened in 1927, according to Linda Kreindler of the Historic Cincinnati Facebook group, who cited the newspaper the *American Israelite*. Castle Farm was razed in 1964.

In 1962, talk turned to those Surf Club competitors who thought that not being located in a bowling alley would be a plus. Dale Stevens reported that a swank supper club could be built on top of the Vernon Manor Hotel in Corryville, and he said that Cincinnati native Doris Day might return to be its opening act. This didn't happen. The hotel, which did host some live entertainment in its lounges and was where big-name acts like the Beatles stayed, closed in 2009. The building now houses the offices for Cincinnati Children's Hospital.

There were, however, two strong attempts to broaden Cincinnati's premier club business. Restaurateur Ben Comisar announced his plans to turn a portion of his Colony Restaurant in Bond Hill's Swifton Shopping Center into a swank entertainment spot that would become active after dinner was over. And though this plan did not last long, Comisar did bring in a number of nationally known comics. One was an antic performer who was then building a name for himself as "the crying comedian": Rip Taylor. He would eventually become famous as a manic, confetti-spraying entertainer before passing away in 2019.

Another effort, Club Diplomat in Walnut Hills, hung around for quite a while, although not as the top-flight destination that its owner, E.S. Hamblen, had hoped for. The club was located in the Kemper Lane Hotel, which was built as a one-hundred-unit apartment hotel in 1922, in spaces that were, at one time, known as the Spa and the Ten-Strike Cocktail Lounge. The establishment had a lovely entrance at 2500 Kemper Lane, with a horseshoe-shaped driveway surrounding a small park. The hotel also boasted storefronts on East McMillan Street. The owners went all in on the renovations to allow for comfortable viewing and dining that could accommodate several hundred patrons. They hired an experienced name in Cincinnati's entertainment business, Colonel Joe Goetz, to book talent, produce shows and handle public relations.

To open on September 20, Goetz called on former lieutenant Steve Rossi, whom he knew from handling talent shows for the U.S. Air Force. The comedy team of Marty Allen and Steve Rossi had been around for a few years, even playing Beverly Hills, and they had essentially become the new Dean Martin and Jerry Lewis. In 1962, they were signed on for six visits to TV's popular *Gary Moore Show*. Rossi was the handsome singer and straight man, and Allen was an irrepressible comedian who resembled a cross between Peter Lorre and Harpo Marx. Opening with Allen and Rossi was a big deal for Club Diplomat.

"Marty is a bug-eyed mop-haired fellow with a fantastic comedy face and the awareness to go with it," Stevens wrote in his review. "He thinks on his feet and can suddenly toss in a line such as 'Jackie Mason just got hit by a bowling ball.'" (Mason was playing the Surf Club, located in Western Bowl, the same night that Allen and Rossi opened.) Allen could also deftly skewer right-wing groups; in one bit, he was introduced as "John Birch" and shouted, "The unknown soldier is a commie." The John Birch Society was a highly visible, paranoid right-wing extremist group of the time that believed America was bedeviled by communist infiltration at the highest levels of society. Allen was also funny off the stage—at the Vernon Manor, a woman stopped him and asked if he was Harpo Marx. "That's my father," he quipped.

According to Stevens, the two were a great start, but attendance slipped with the next two acts: singer Kitty Kallen ("My Coloring Book") and the distinguished sixty-six-year-old British-born actor of American films and stage shows Alan Mowbray. He played George Washington in the 1931 film *Alexander Hamilton*. Mowbray's one-night appearance at Club Diplomat on October 4 was one for the ages—in a perverse way. "You had to be there," Stevens wrote of Mowbray's opening—and closing—night. "It was really something in showbiz annals last night at Club Diplomat. Actor Alan Mowbray was the headline act, and he did 11 minutes, which may be a new world's record for headline brevity....To put it kindly, he came across as a luncheon club toastmaster, and his jokes were not new, nor were they funny." Stevens did note one interesting anecdote Mowbray told: Richard Nixon's wife, Pat, had been a dancer in his 1935 movie *Becky Sharp*. And Stevens praised the opening act, singer Sheila Reynolds.

After the audience failed to laugh at the jokes, Mowbray quickly called it quits. His booking was canceled, and he left Cincinnati, giving up on his professional stand-up routine. Mowbray did have some further success on Broadway before dying in 1972. (I don't know if his gravestone says, "All things considered, I'd rather be in Cincinnati.")

Club Diplomat's remaining time as a swank nightclub was troubled. At one point, the owners sued Stevens and the *Post* for defamation after a column intimated that it would soon close. (The lawsuits were dismissed.) In mid-November, Hamblen announced that he was suspending the big-name headliners and cover charge and emphasizing dining, dancing and entertainment. He also announced the hiring of Bert Pichel, a local entertainer known as Professor Puff Puff, as the head of public relations.

Club Diplomat continued to show up in newspapers. In August 1963, it hosted the *Jewel Box Revue* of "female impersonators who strip." The last clip I found was from October 13, 1975, when political activist Penny Maines arrived to talk to fellow Democrats about Bobbie Sterne's campaign for city council. (Sterne was a popular vote-getter who also served as mayor.) Maines found herself talking to Republicans—she had the wrong night. "It seems that on Monday night, the Republicans meet at Club Diplomat, and on Tuesday, the Democrats meet there," she told the *Post*.

Meanwhile, it was never easy for the Surf Club, either. It tried novelty programming, such as Turkish belly dancers. Like other clubs, it tried emphasizing, for a time, brief costumes "to show their waitresses off to best advantage," as the *Enquirer*'s Luke Feck reported in November 1962.

One problem was television's growing popularity. Live acts that were benefiting from TV exposure were raising their prices. In 1963, the *Enquirer* reported, the Surf Club filed a $50,000 damage suit in United States District Court against Frank Fontaine, a veteran comic who had recently become a big star portraying the inebriated Crazy Guggenheim on *The Jackie Gleason Show*'s "Joe the Bartender" segments. His gimmick was having his drunken character break into ballads, sung in a beautifully sweet voice, and America loved the sentimental surprise of it.

In October 1962, according to the *Enquirer* and *Post*, Fontaine signed a contract to play the Surf Club the next June for $4,000. But in the meantime, he had issued an album of songs that was a massive hit. As a result, he asked for an additional $3,500; after not getting it, he canceled by telegram. Eventually, Fontaine paid his union $4,000, which it gave to Hoinke to settle matters. But the damage was done. According to Russell Hoinke, who was born in 1961, his dad told him years later that the Fontaine experience helped him decide to close the Surf Club as a showroom in September 1963. "Dad said he loved it, but it got to where it started to be such a pain, it wasn't worth doing it."

On October 17, 1963, the Surf Club's billiard parlor opened with a guest appearance and demonstration by Jimmy Caras, who was advertised as a four-time billiard champion. The Surf Club as a top-flight nightclub was short-lived but rolled a number of strikes with its bookings.

4

DOWNTOWN CINCINNATI

*W*hen the Beverly Hills Supper Club ceased its large floor shows, Dale Stevens wrote in the *Cincinnati Post* on October 16, 1961, that the Living Room downtown might become its replacement. (He also touted the Surf Club in Western Hills.) And he was right about that, as the Living Room managed to last until 1970 as a beacon of downtown's Swinging Sixties entertainment scene. However, Stevens was speculating when he wrote the story—only two weeks earlier, he had reported that the Living Room would soon be opening, so he hadn't yet seen much of the place in action.

The Living Room was originally located at 515 Walnut Street. It was next to the Keith's Theatre, one of downtown's many beautiful movie palaces that are now all gone, to our everlasting civic regret. The club was originally called the Piano Lounge and was owned by pianist Herman Kirschner. And it was the kind of fun place you'd expect it to be with a title like that. "Performers in the stage musicals that come to the Shubert [Theatre] regularly beat a path to the Piano Lounge," Stevens wrote in 1958. "Herman Kirschner, who plays all their songs via his piano, recalls that the cast from *Fanny* did 'almost their whole show' while gathered around his piano." (*Fanny* debuted on Broadway in 1954 and was based on a novel by Marcel Pagnol about love and life in the French seaport city of Marseille.)

Kirschner owned the club until Mel Herman, whose record industry businesses included a retail store and a distribution company, announced his purchase in October 1961. As a distributor, Herman had helped the

Cincinnati label Fraternity Records move thirty thousand copies of Jimmy Dorsey's 1957 "So Rare" locally, playing a key role in it becoming a surprise national hit for the big band leader. Herman's plans were to make the Piano Lounge a "plush music spot" called the Living Room and to bring in national piano jazz trios on the order of those led by Ahmad Jamal, Ramsey Lewis, Teddy Wilson and Erroll Garner (of "Misty" fame). To do that, Herman promised a major renovation, with sofa seating on tiered levels accommodating 110 people. He also promised to serve lunch and evening dinners, offering such upscale entrées as steak and lobster.

It seems the club used both names for a while. Stevens wrote on January 3, 1962, that the place was packed nightly "and its $35,000 redecorating job, with Brazilian rosewood and a 'stoned' bar, will be completed soon." At the time, the club advertised the nationally known trumpeter Don Goldie and his quintet. (Goldie worked with trombonist Jack Teagarden, although he would later collaborate with the rockers Sir Douglas Quintet on their beautiful instrumental "We'll Take Our Last Walk Tonight.") Herman also had a house vocalist, Judy James, and a house band, the hardworking local favorites the Dee Felice Trio, featuring Felice on drums.

Herman booked an impressive variety of acts at the Living Room until the end came. Pat Kelly's and Bill Soudrette's Cincinnati Jazz Hall of History website (www.patkellymusic.com) has compiled a list of its acts—it was quite an accomplishment. The club's veteran and upcoming jazz players included Dizzy Gillespie, Duke Ellington, the Coleman Hawkins Quartet, the Ramsey Lewis Trio, guitarist extraordinaire Wes Montgomery, stylish flutist Herbie Mann and saxophonist Cannonball Adderley. It also brought in some of the best vocalists of the decade, including Dakota Stanton; Johnny Hartman; Jackie Paris, with Anne Marie Moss; Betty Carter; and Carmen McRae. Herman also experimented, trying Brazilian-influenced pop and jazz with Sergio Mendes & Brasil '66 and the Xavier Cugat Orchestra (with Charo); blues and soul with B.B. King, Maxine Brown and the Drifters; comedy with Redd Foxx and Flip Wilson; and even hypnotism.

Herman's support of local acts as headliners included vocal stylist Amanda Ambrose and Curtis Peagler's Modern Jazz Disciples, a group that played widely and was pegged for national success. Eddie "Lockjaw" Davis, a powerful and respected saxophonist, had signed them to New Jazz, a subsidiary of the major label Prestige Records, and they released two albums in 1959 and 1960 with Peagler on sax and William Kelley playing a valve trombone shaped like an alto sax and called a normaphone—plus a pianist, bassist and drumer.

In 2001, those records were combined and reissued on Fantasy Records as *Disciple Blues*. Reviewing the disc for the All About Jazz website, Derek Taylor wrote:

> *Discs like this one are among the most fascinating and enjoyable in the voluminous Fantasy jazz oeuvre; artifacts from forgotten groups who were left by the wayside of popular notice, not because of any absence of talent or creativity, but simply because they surfaced during a time when jazz was rife with staggering amounts of both. In an era when more modern jazz giants walked the earth and were actively recording than at any other time, it must have been a sobering prospect for fledgling groups like this one to find an audience.*

Things didn't always go smoothly at the Living Room's shows. In December 1962, a brouhaha erupted when singer Carmen McRae got mad at the chatty audience. The *Post*'s Stevens reported that "her unhappiness stemmed from throngs not always quiet, particularly annoying to her because of the show rooms she normally plays. Tuesday night, she told off the customers in no uncertain terms, took a long intermission and did her final show sitting at the stage counter, facing away from the patrons." Herman told Stevens he was not going to book singers anymore because of the noisy crowds, but in time, he relented.

Walnut Street in the early to mid-1960s was a sizzling, cosmopolitan urban strip full of nightlife. In addition to the Living Room/Piano Lounge, there was also the Blue Angel at 608 Walnut, the Penthouse in the basement of the Metropole Hotel at 609 Walnut, the Apartment at 620 Walnut and the Barn and the Hangar—twin but separate establishments—at 625 Walnut.

In late November 1964, the *Post* printed a memorable story about the adventures of a young couple, Dave and Joyce Burns, who won an all-expenses-paid night on the town, courtesy of Robert Elkus, the owner of Dino's, downtown's prestigious high-fashion clothing store. The Burnses went to seven entertainment venues situated within two blocks of each other—those mentioned previously, along with the Kasbah in the basement of the Terrace Hilton Hotel (where pianist Jimmy Ryan entertained) and the brand-new Playboy Club on the top floor of the Executive Building at 35 East Seventh Street (at Walnut), where Joyce found even the restroom dazzling. At the Hangar, the couple heard pianist/singer Mildred Wilson, who reminded them of Bessie Smith and was "a living testimonial to that which was heard in the great blues era of the 1910s and '20s." At the separate Barn, Mousy Melvin's Quartet entertained. Over at the Blue Angel, the couple mostly liked the great R&B singer and pianist Amos Milburn, known for his earthy drinking songs like "Bad, Bad Whiskey" and "One Scotch, One Bourbon, One Beer." (The Blue Angel, by the way, experienced numerous transformations. It ran a discotheque format by 1965; by the early 1970s, it had become Larry Flynt's Hustler Club. The Aronoff Center for the Arts now sits in the space.)

The Burnses enjoyed the dreamy vocal group the Flamingos (performers of the timeless "I Only Have Eyes for You") at the Living Room, but they were left unmoved by modernist jazz pianist Thelonious Monk at the Penthouse. At the Apartment, the Prince Carr Trio played. "They did have some jazz, an organ player," remembered Lou Lausche about the Apartment. As a young bassist (and law student) in Cincinnati in the early 1960s, Lausche frequented the clubs. "It was more of a girlie joint—that's how I remember it. It was very small, smoky, dark."

The Burnses' fabulous night on the town was meant to prove to all that Cincinnati was jumping late into the night with quality live music, especially jazz. Once the Ohio Valley Jazz Festival got underway in 1962, there was a growing and increasingly sophisticated audience for touring musicians, as well as loyal support for locals. The city was also home to King Records and a community of professional musicians who supported its stars, such as James Brown and Hank Ballard, then in the vanguard of soul music.

Of course, not all downtown clubs were situated on Walnut Street. Although it petered out in the early 1960s, the Cat & Fiddle, located at 217 West Fifth Street (one block west of the Netherland, as its advertisements touted), mixed "girlie shows" with an orchestra, an organist and low-priced dinners. The club did sharp business in 1955 with Lady Godiva and her trained horse, Melody Lane. They stayed for three weeks. (The Lady Godiva schtick must have been a great gimmick for nightclubs. In 1939, an act called Lady Godiva and Her 7 Peeping Toms came direct from Detroit to the Peebles Corner Nite Club in Walnut Hills.)

Several big hotels, now long gone, contained lounges that featured all manner of music. The Sinton Hotel's Coal Hole presented singer/pianist Shirley Jester, one of the era's top names in local musical talent. The Sheraton-Gibson Hotel's Rathskeller, at one point, offered Gene Redd & His Peppermint Twisters, plus music from Barney Rapp. That probably would have been a great place to twist—those musicians sure had impressive histories. Redd was King Records' music director, played trumpet and vibraphone and was in the band that recorded James Brown's essential 1963 King album *Live at the Apollo*.

Rapp was a seasoned big-band and orchestra leader, as well as a beloved local celebrity. He was active on WLW's popular *50-50 Club* television show hosted by Ruth Lyons. He also once owned a club in Paddock Hills called the Sign of the Drum, which was where he met singer Ruby Wright. They married in 1937. When pregnancy stopped Wright from performing in 1939, Rapp hired a relatively unknown local replacement named Doris Kappelhoff. According to a John Kiesewetter report for WVXU-FM in 2017, Rapp thought Doris should choose a shorter last name and suggested "Day." It stuck.

The Sheraton's Yeatman's Cove, at one point, presented Capitol Records recording artist Will Mercer. Who exactly Mercer was isn't clear, but there was, at that time, a Will Mercer who recorded for his own label, a bluesy Bobby Darin–style crooner whose "Just a Nobody" still sounds good today. And while there were probably few, if any, people who went to the Gayety Burlesque on Vine Street just for the comedy or the music, it drew crowds—sex does that.

Speaking of sex, the Playboy Club was where "bunnies," wearing brief outfits, served customers food and drinks while musicians and comedians performed. The Cincinnati outpost of the series of key clubs started by *Playboy* magazine founder Hugh Hefner was announced at the end of 1963 and opened in March 1964. The *Post*'s Stevens reported that Playboy had signed a ten-year lease, probably for $30,000 per year, on the thirteen-thousand-square-foot top floor of the eight-story building. The club would have two showrooms, a bar, special lounges for bunnies and performers, service quarters and a seamstress's room. It was definitely out to raise the bar of downtown entertainment spots.

But when Stevens wrote about those just-announced plans, he quoted the Playboy Club's Victor Lownes as being worried about community resistance. "Little old ladies can't believe the bunnies are around just to give good service," Lownes said. And the club did draw some protests when it opened in Cincinnati, but it was also cheered as a breakthrough against the city's puritanism. By the time it closed in 1983, the Cincinnati Playboy Club and the Playboy brand itself were becoming anachronistic for their male-centric idealization of conventionally "sexy" female stereotypes in the face of the women's liberation movement.

I wrote about that problem in 1981, when the *Enquirer* assigned me to attend a tryout for future *Playboy* magazine Playmates at the club. "What kind of Cincinnati woman likes *Playboy*?" I wrote:

> *She lives in a log cabin with outdoor plumbing, has a pet boa constrictor and earns money by sewing uniforms for men to wear during re-enactments of Civil War battles. That description covers Paulette Plunkett, one of 120 young women to answer Playboy magazine's call for a Cincinnati playmate—a playmate being the female who poses for Playboy's monthly centerfold photo feature, invariably in the nude.*
>
> *This search is a test to see if Playboy can more easily reduce the preponderance of blonde-haired, California-girl, bathing beauty–type playmates—all the "10s." Indeed, the last Ohio playmate appeared in 1976—and she had moved to California first.*

All of the clubs are gone; the magazine ceased publication in 2020.

In the 1960s, downtown also saw the occasional musical special event in an unconventional locale. As one example, well ahead of the British Invasion that started in 1964, English rock star Cliff Richard and his band, the Shadows, appeared on stage at the RKO Palace movie theater on October 24, 1962, the night Richard's film *Wonderful to Be Young* opened. Promoted with the tagline "That singin' guy in a most swingin' affair," it was a bid to present Richard in America as an Elvis-like pop and film star. But he'd have to wait another fourteen years to have his first U.S. top 10 hit, "Devil Woman."

As another example, Jackie Wilson—no stranger to traditional local concert venues—did two Saturday night shows at an offbeat location for him, the three-thousand-seat Albee Theatre on Fountain Square, on April 8, 1967. He sold out the 11:00 p.m. show and came close to selling out the 8:00 p.m. performance. Wilson had some amazing support: Howard Tate, who sang his original version of "Get It While You Can," a song Janis Joplin later made more famous; Freddie Scott; B.B. King; the Drifters; Big Maybelle; and a dancer/acrobat named Peg Leg Moffitt.

And the Miss Teen-Age Cincinnati Extravaganza at the Sheraton-Gibson Hotel on October 2, 1965, chose a then-little-known out-of-town rock band for its festivities—Paul Revere and the Raiders. The band was just weeks away from "Just Like Me," their first of many million-selling rock 'n' roll hits. The *Post* used the occasion to let its fifty-seven high school correspondents interview the band upon their arrival at Greater Cincinnati Airport.

Incidentally, the Raiders may not have had any big hits yet, but they had acquired a reputation on the bar circuit for their wild live shows and hustling work ethic, and they capitalized on that in Cincinnati. As soon as their 8:00 p.m. Miss Teen-Age Cincinnati dance was over, they rushed to Newport's Flamingo Club for three shows—at 10:00 p.m., midnight and 2:00 a.m.

It's no wonder that, amid such a lively downtown musical environment, Herman's Living Room did well. In early 1965, it was announced that Herman would move his Living Room to the first floor of the Metropole Hotel, barely one block away. Further, there would be a $250,000 renovation to create what Dale Stevens called "a fancy supper club." Herman had taken out a fifteen-year lease on the space. The move was prompted by the city, as it wanted to tear down his existing club for urban renewal that, given all the happening nightlife, probably wasn't needed. (The space is now part of the Fifth Third Center development at Fountain Square Plaza.)

"It was big enough to hold a big band and be comfortable, and it had Stan Kenton and Woody Herman," Lausche said of the new location. "It was a very fancy, nice club." A potential problem for the new Living Room was that the Metropole already had the Penthouse in its basement, which was run by musician Dee Felice and WNOP personality Dick Pike and also brought in big-name jazz acts. These acts included the young, destined-for-fame trumpeter Freddie Hubbard; droll singer-pianist Mose Allison; soul-jazz organist Brother Jack McDuff; and the phenomenal multi-instrumentalist Roland Kirk. But that potential conflict was resolved in advance—the Penthouse closed at the end of 1964, replaced by the trendy Whiskey-A-Go-Go Discotheque. (After that, it gets hard to track what went in and out of the Metropole basement in the 1960s—names like the Trip and Tommy Helms's Dugout pop up.)

The new Living Room's start was rocky. Canadian pianist Oscar Peterson missed his plane for the September 9, 1965 opening, but he was there the next night, according to the *Post*. Herman hoped to have the new Living Room feature the Ramsey Lewis Trio, then enjoying national success with its jazzy instrumental version of the pop song "The In Crowd." But he wound up having to switch Lewis to his older, smaller club, only to have the hot musician cancel due to an injury. The old Living Room/Piano Lounge ultimately closed with the Cuban percussionist and bandleader Mongo Santamaria, whose 1962 Herbie Hancock–penned hit "Watermelon Man" was already on its way to becoming a Latin jazz milestone.

The new Living Room's initial bookings were trumpeter Maynard Ferguson, singer Mark Murphy and piano-based trio the Three Sounds (who sometimes used the numeral "3" instead of "three"). The latter had sentimental significance, as they had released a *Live at the Living Room* album in 1964.

Initially, visiting the Living Room was as much about seeing the place as the bands. "That bright, new, inviting front you see on the bright, new, inviting Living Room is a portent of what you'll find inside," read the *Cincinnati Enquirer* on November 27, 1965. "Be prepared for an entirely different 'look' to that familiar old Living Room, now at 609 Walnut Street in the Metropole Hotel. They started from scratch here, and the enticing décor includes plush carpeting, crystal chandeliers and many little details you can't comprehend all at once. But the overall effect is one of quiet elegance that continues on through the prime jazz entertainment that proprietor Mel Herman always has on hand," the *Enquirer* article explained. "The 'Room' is semi-divided after you leave the foyer, with a delightful lounge adjacent to the bar, then a beautiful restaurant area. A little beyond this is the 'jazz heaven,' where you can enjoy both the entertainment and the potables. There's a cover charge here but not for those partaking of the excellent food in the dining room." That food, according to a Living Room advertisement, included special $5.50 meals, featuring such entrees as African lobster tails, filet mignon, pompano del casa and twin tournedos with Bordelaise sauce. (Wine cost $0.85 extra.)

In November 1965, the Living Room experimented with a supper-club-friendly booking of a singer and comedian. Stevens, in a review, said such an approach fit better with its new upscale environs than "hard jazz." Alas, he said, the acts—singer Joya Sherrill and comedian Flip Wilson—"were routine rather than inspiring." He liked Wilson's material but not his low-key presentation.

Sherrill, I'm afraid, has been lost to posterity—she was a jazz singer who, as a teenager, performed with Duke Ellington and had a lovely voice, as evidenced by her songs that are available on YouTube. But Flip Wilson emerged as a top comedian. At the Living Room, he gave an early performance of one of his hippest routines, "Columbus," which would be included on his 1967 album *Cowboys and Colored People*. Wilson's skewed reworking of Christopher Columbus's "discovery" of America—where Queen Isabella wants him to go so that he'll discover Ray Charles, and the Natives yell nasty things about his mother to get him to leave—would become a well-regarded 1960s comedy routine.

Toward its later years, the Living Room presented hypnotist Traian Boyer. He was impressive, according to one of the patrons he hypnotized, Tim

Swallow (now of Cincinnati World Cinema). "A very interesting experience," Swallow remembered in an email:

> *I did not feel a sensation of going under but was later told that I, too, sat in a chair asleep for a few minutes, of which I had no recollection. I do remember the end of the dance steps with the two men—but had no idea how I got there. Inexplicably, at the time, I found myself wanting to do the soft-shoe, although I had never done it before.*
>
> *So, I came to believe that hypnosis and the power of planted suggestion works. Based on that experience, many years later, I went through hypnosis to stop smoking, and it worked for six months.*

The end came very quietly to the Living Room in early 1970. As fate would have it, Stevens had just returned to Cincinnati from three and a half years as a *Detroit News* editor and was then writing for the *Enquirer* as its amusements editor. In his introductory "Back Home—Again!" column bout Cincinnati's nightlife, he displayed sadness about Walnut Street's decline. "Walnut Street is dimmer," he wrote. "The Living Room, where I once did a radio show, is closed. It might even become a lunch-time restaurant. The old Blue Angel is something else now. The Apartment no longer has music. Sure, there still are the itinerant girls. But the street is strangely less active, and it bothers me." (He didn't explain what he meant by "itinerant girls.")

Herman died in 1990 at the age of sixty-eight after a long illness. In his obituary, Cincinnati jazz drummer Ron McCurdy, who played at the Living Room, remembered him this way: "I never heard a musician say a bad word about him, which was rare for a club owner. He was a much-beloved cat."

5

SEVEN CITIES

*S*even Cities Coffee House, near the University of Cincinnati's campus, brought home the spirit of the early 1960s folk revival. That was a time when pop-oriented folk groups like the Kingston Trio and Peter, Paul and Mary were having hit singles and selling albums to college-age audiences, while more roots-minded folk performers like Dave Van Ronk, Fred Neil and a young Bob Dylan were coming up, and the iconic Pete Seeger was looking on all the revived interest approvingly. It was also a time of discovering roots in music; Appalachian folk ballads, bluegrass and the blues were finding increasing acceptance as college students (and some high schoolers) wanted more sophisticated music than teen rock and more relevant voices than the pop crooners of their parents.

The *Cincinnati Post*'s entertainment editor Dale Stevens introduced the new Seven Cities to his reading public on September 30, 1960, after the *Post* had first announced that it was coming. "Conservative Cincinnati gets its first legitimate coffee house this week when the Seven Cities opens tomorrow at 5:30 p.m. at Calhoun and Dennis near the UC campus," he wrote. "The exotic spot, named for its alcoves furnished in the manner of such cities as Madrid and Tokyo, is owned by Jules Rosen and Lee Dorfman, who spent months examining similar coffee houses in New York and Chicago." Stevens continued with a description that makes Seven Cities seem like a portal to our present day, when there's at least one imaginatively designed, indie-spirited hip coffee house in every town:

It also has an extensive menu of genuine foreign coffees, teas and tidbits, including German soup, Peruvian coffee, Russian tea and soft drinks made from imported Italian syrups. Pastries, meats, cheeses and breads also will be available.

If you had seen the place, as I did, in its original form as a garage, the transformation would seem remarkable. One alcove, with sand on the floor (you have to take off your shoes) is a Polynesian Room. The Greenwich Village corner has a stage for a model and special "palette" seats for the artists.

(While Stevens called the 3,500-square-foot basement space a former garage, other sources referred to it as a former tire store and a place with horse stalls.)

It should be noted that one can go too far in marveling at the progressivism of any entertainment venue in 1960. Seven Cities Continental Coffee House placed a newspaper advertisement ahead of its opening that read, in part, "Need attractive neat girls between 18 and 25, for waitress hostesses, full or part time."

Seven Cities was more than a thematically cosmopolitan place for drinks and light meals, appealing to those who wished to daydream about being artists or models. Until it closed in late 1963, it also had open music sessions on Wednesday nights—"hootenanny" was the term in favor then—to let the city's budding folk performers hone their skills and perhaps become Seven Cities regulars. And it had other innovative live entertainment: jazz, Afro-Cuban drummers, international fashion shows, and Broadway actor and original Playhouse in the Park company member (and future *Magnum, P.I.* star) John Hillerman even offered dramatic and humorous readings. Seven Cities also provided an outlet for a then-new entertainment form coming out of New York's off-Broadway scene and Chicago's Second City—improv comedy. This happened in 1962, when Davy Jones (the first director at Playhouse in the Park), Sue Lawless and Herb Sufrin presented their *Highly Improbable* revue at the club to a strong response.

Matthew Knott Johnson, a young singer and University of Cincinnati student when Seven Cities opened (he was an opening-night act), recalled spending time there even when he wasn't performing. *Highly Improbable* was a favorite of his. "They took the beginning line from someone in the audience, the ending line from someone else and a theme from someone else, then huddled together and came up with stuff," he said. "They were well ahead of their time."

Lee "Leon" Dorfman emerged quickly as the coffeehouse's most visible figure. A Hughes High School graduate who died in 2019, he was an outsized character. His obituary, which doesn't mention Seven Cities, chronicled his narrow escape while he serving as a U.S. Merchant Marine radio operator in World War II aboard the USS *Henry Miller*. He was returning to the United States from the Gibraltar naval base on January 3, 1945, when the ship was torpedoed by a German U-boat. "The *Miller* began to list severely, [and] the captain ordered the crew to abandon ship. Lee volunteered to return to the ship as part of a skeleton crew. After the crew got control of flooding in the cargo holds, the *Henry Miller* was able to limp back to port," the obituary read.

Dorfman remained a boat buff even as he developed a taste for folk music. In February 1961, the *Cincinnati Enquirer*'s outdoors columnist Bob Rankin interviewed him about a new venture—becoming a Cincinnati distributor for German-made Klepper folding boats. Dorfman announced that he would display the boat on the upper floor of Seven Cities every night from 6:00 p.m. to midnight while folk songs flowed from the basement below. "This is a real good item for the family that wants to go boating but who live in an apartment," Dorfman told Rankin. "They can easily store the boat on a shelf when not in use." (Klepper's hand-crafted folding kayaks are still made in Germany.)

Familiar local performers appeared at Seven Cities. One was Cincinnati jazz vocal stylist Popeye Maupin; another was singer Lydia Wood. Later in the decade, as times became more wigged-out and strange, Wood became known for working with Cincinnati Joe as "Mad Lydia" and recorded songs like "Madam Satan." In 1972, the duo opened a club in the subterranean level of the Netherland Hilton Hotel called Catacomb Hideaway that was decorated with a witch motif.

Others who played at Seven Cities went on to be active in the Queen City Balladeers, which formed in 1963 and was still meeting weekly at its Leo Coffeehouse inside Norwood's Zion United Church of Christ when the 2020 COVID-19 pandemic struck.

Seven Cities did launch the notable professional career of Danny Cox, who started singing there while he was still at Walnut Hills High School. He went on to be a folk/rock recording artist on nationally distributed labels. And in Cox's adopted home of Kansas City, he has been an actor and playwright who wrote the music and lyrics for and appeared in the theatrical production *Fair Ball*, which tells the story of baseball's Negro Leagues. (The Negro Leagues Baseball Museum is located in Kansas City.)

Popular local musician Popeye Maupin in a 1978 *Enquirer* illustration by Laslo Vespremi. *Courtesy of the* Cincinnati Enquirer.

Cox's talent was recognized quickly at Seven Cities. His voice was memorable—both sweetly gentle and, when it needed to be, powerfully expressive. Dorfman released a 1962 album by the young singer called *Live at 7 Cities* on the Seven Cities label, with liner notes by journalist Stevens. As a Walnut Hills student, Cox had already had experience with the protest songs of the 1950s, having been involved in local civil rights movements, especially the long struggle to integrate the Coney Island Amusement Park and its Sunlite Pool, since the eighth grade. He had also developed a knowledge of political activist music through his high school friend John Sweet, a guitarist and singer whose father, Fred, edited a labor union newspaper, and mother, Mary Allen, was a political progressive. (Fred Sweet was one of the interviewees in Studs Terkel's best-selling book *Hard Times: An Oral History of the Great Depression*.) "All the left-wing folksingers going through town would stop at John's house, people like Pete Seeger," recalled Cox, in an interview for this book. "I got into folk music on the political side with those guys."

Before Seven Cities, Cox frequently performed with Sweet and a third Walnut Hills student, the aforementioned Matthew Knott Johnson, at events sponsored by the youth program of Fellowship House of Cincinnati. Sweet was White; Knott Johnson, like Cox, was Black. (Born Matthew Johnson, Matthew took his stepfather's name, Knott, in high school but reverted to Matthew Johnson for graduation and now uses both surnames.)

Cincinnati's Fellowship House was an innovative local organization, dedicated to encouraging racial understanding and integration. It was started in Cincinnati in the 1940s as a project of the Woman's City Club. The club's members had heard Marjorie Penny of Baltimore talk about the national movement. The late Cincinnati civil rights leader and city council member Marian A. Spencer—the third president of Cincinnati's Fellowship House—discussed it in her memoir *Keep on Fighting: The Life and Civil Rights Legacy of Marian A. Spencer*, written by Dorothy H. Christenson:

> *Fellowship House sponsored monthly lunch meetings for local priests, pastors, and rabbis, and had three action sections: Trios, the Doll Project and a mixed-race Fellowship House Choir. Trios were groups of three—a Caucasian, a Negro and a Jew—who spoke about all things we had in common. They spoke wherever requested: to school classrooms, Parent Teacher Associations and assemblies, church groups of all ages and community council meetings. There were sixty trios, including ten made up of honor students at Walnut Hills High School. The group was listed*

at the public library's speakers' bureau, and they were kept busy, as racial tensions in the city were high. The integrated choir performed often and sometimes along with a Trio for a community program.

According to Cincinnati Museum Center records, *Post* stories and also using Spencer's account, Fellowship House lasted until 1969. For a time, it was headquartered in an old mansion on Lexington Avenue in Avondale that had been given to the Cincinnati Park Board by the John Z. Herschede family—he was president of the National Underwriter Company and part of the family known for owning downtown's Herschede Jewelers.

Firebombed during the civil disturbances of 1967, the house was eventually torn down to make room for a park. "Fellowship House never recovered from the disaster, probably because the White and Jewish membership were afraid to come to Avondale after the riots," Spencer said in her book. But before its end, Fellowship House had strong support at Walnut Hills High School. It presented the destined-for-greatness blues and folk singer Odetta there on March 12, 1961, the same year that Reverend Martin Luther King Jr. called her "the Queen of American Folk Music."

Cox, Sweet and Knott Johnson were close to another Walnut Hills student and Fellowship House activist, Nancy Felson. They would sometimes gather at her North Avondale home with other Fellowship House students to sing. "Basically, it was like a hootenanny," recalled Felson, now a retired classics professor in Athens, Georgia. She said they would sing "900 Miles," "Dark as a Dungeon" (a song about the dangers of coal mining written by Merle Travis, who also wrote "16 Tons") and "There Once Was a Union Maid" (a pro-union song written by Woody Guthrie). "Danny and Matthew used to sing 'Danny Boy' to me. I was just blown away by it," she said.

Knott Johnson, who came from a financially struggling family, found those gatherings blissful. "It was just such a beautiful thing to mix and mend and love," he said. "That was such an overflow of joy and loving and appreciating one another. I was just touched by the openness and the learning of different cultures, the different people appreciating one another."

Cox said he didn't yet realize such songs were "folk" per se. So, he wasn't sure what to expect the first time he went to Seven Cities with Sweet and Knott Johnson shortly after it opened. "I went there in high school to see what a beatnik looked like, and they were having open mic," he recalled. "John said, 'Why don't you get up and sing something?' I said, 'I don't know any folk songs.' And he said, 'Well, all those protest songs we sang *are* folk songs.' So, I got up with them and [Dorfman] said, 'Why don't you boys come back next week, and I'll pay you?' You actually pay people for this? I couldn't believe it."

Once Seven Cities opened, Cox quickly became a local sensation and its signature musical act—not just as part of a trio with Sweet and Johnson but also as a soloist. Cox also began to play elsewhere, but Seven Cities was his home base. Meanwhile, he transferred to Withrow High School for his senior year. (Debbie Heldman, the executive director of Walnut Hills High School's Alumni Foundation, said via email that "the class of 1961 considers him a part of their class; he has come to reunions, so we are proud of him.")

In a September 24, 1961 *Enquirer* article, writer John Cannon described a Cox show at Seven Cities. "A blue spotlight ringed the features of a young Negro seated on a piano stool in the middle of a small stage. He strummed a guitar softly. 'Good evening, ladies and gentlemen. Welcome to the Seven Cities.' Danny Cox, 18-year-old graduate of Withrow High School, then began to sing." Cannon sampled Cox's repertoire—"Venezuela," "Shenandoah," a Spanish folk song and "Railroad Bill." "The audience at Seven Cities Coffee House loved it," he noted.

The *Live at 7 Cities* album that Cox recorded for Dorfman features folk and protest songs like "We Shall Overcome," "House of the Rising Sun," "John Henry" and "Nobody Knows You When You're Down and Out." It also includes "Danny Boy," a favorite of Cox's fans. The album featured liner notes from journalist Stevens, who described Cox's "instant success" at Seven Cities. "Lee was a good guy," Cox says of Dorfman. "Lee wanted to do the album and so did Dale Stevens, who said, 'Man, let's get this record out.'" It was recorded in the summer of 1961.

Seven Cities' years overlapped with the national popularity of the *hootenanny*, a colloquial term for a party that had slowly come to signify an informal gathering of song-sharing folk singers. That use of the word began in the early 1940s—according to Wikipedia—when Pete Seeger and Woody Guthrie used it to describe their New York rent parties. And it gained widespread use when pop-style folk songs became hits in the early 1960s, an idealistic era. In Cincinnati, WKRC-TV even broadcast a local *Hoot-Innati* show featuring local talent. And a nightclub in Northern Kentucky, Black Orchid, even tried a "Boozenanny" night. In 1963–64, an ABC network music variety show called *Hootenanny* featured folk musicians of the day. Infamously, however, network officials wouldn't let Seeger appear due to his past Communist Party sympathies. As a result, many of the biggest folk acts, such as Peter, Paul and Mary; the Kingston Trio; Joan Baez; and Phil Ochs, boycotted the show.

But since the word *hootenanny* was an established folk music term long before the ABC show, a number of promoters put together their own hootenanny concert tours that owed nothing to the show but could piggyback on its popularity. There were so many, they probably bumped into each other at highway rest stops. Cox was involved with one of them, *Hootenanny '63*, which was initially operated by Progressive Promotions from a Cincinnati address. "We had my sister, who sang; I did my show and did an homage or parody of the television show," Cox said. "And there was a comedic folk-singing group, a serious, young, college-looking group and a bluegrass group. The bluegrass group we had was the real deal from West Virginia—the Bluegrass Playboys. They were incredible," he said. "My old manager and I owned the tour," Cox explained. "We had a bus parked at my house. So, imagine how these different cultures were living on this bus together. We stayed at the same hotels. There was not one name on the show, but the concept of a hootenanny was so big, and the timing was right. We sold out two shows at Carnegie Hall and had to put 200 people on the stage."

The Carnegie Hall shows seem fantastical in retrospect—how could Cox have gone from Seven Cities to Carnegie Hall so easily? Fortunately, *Billboard*—the national publication devoted to the music industry—covered the August engagement under the headline "No Names at Hoot—Just Lots of Folk." The article marveled at the Friday and Saturday sellouts. (Carnegie Hall's archives list two shows occurring on August 24 but none on August 23, but Cox says there were two each day. Good sales could have generated extra shows.) "Ten unknown acts drew an overflow crowd to New York's Carnegie Hall. The show was billed merely as *Hootenanny '63*, with no mention made in advertising about the performers' identity," *Billboard* reported. "Standouts among the performers included Danny Cox, a folk singer blessed with a rich voice and a love of singing out, whose impressive song insight was matched by his professional stage presence." By then, the show had a larger promoter, Hal Zeigler, and Cox followed him to Los Angeles. What followed for Cox was an interesting and exciting career, if never breakout national stardom, as a singer.

As the market for rock exploded, Cox made more albums with aspirations of finding a national audience, as other contemporary folk-influenced performers had. The cover of his 1966 album, *Sunny*, used electrifying colors and psychedelic lettering; 1969 brought a two-record set called *Birth Announcement*, with a cover featuring Cox in a bathtub, wearing a straw hat. Next came *Live at the Family Dog*, a self-titled album, and *Feel So Good*. The latter found Cox with a glossily produced pop album on Casablanca, the super-hot 1970s label that was home to Kiss, Donna Summer, Parliament and the Village People. By the early 1970s, Cox had established himself in the music business in Kansas City, where he has remained, expanding into theater and other arts.

"I came out from Los Angeles with Brewer & Shipley [a folk duo now known for the classic 1971 hit 'One Toke Over the Line'] to start a company in the Midwest because there were so many colleges," Cox said. He became a partner in Good Karma Productions, which managed him, Brewer & Shipley, the Ozark Mountain Daredevils and others. From 1971 to 1974, Cox co-owned Cowtown Ballroom, Kansas City's equivalent of Ludlow Garage (see chapter 12) and the subject of a PBS documentary, *Cowtown Ballroom...Sweet Jesus*. "Whatever I did, it all brought me to the point where I have a beautiful family—ten children, eighteen grandchildren, and I love them all. My wife is Mona."

Surprisingly, before Seven Cities opened, there was another coffeehouse in Cincinnati—and Knott Johnson and Sweet were part of that one, too. This fact might seem to conflict with what journalist Stevens reported and I quoted earlier—"Conservative Cincinnati gets its first legitimate coffee house this week when the Seven Cities opens." But the key word in that passage is *legitimate*. Earlier in 1960, a place called the Prophet opened in downtown at 704 Main Street with orange-and-white parachute draping, a Buddha incense burner and a seventy-four-year-old espresso machine. Stevens didn't like the Prophet much; he called it a "pseudo-beatnik showcase attended more by the tourist trade than those sincerely in search of good entertainment." And its owner, Royce Adams, probably didn't help win over Stevens when he told another *Post* columnist, Si Cornell, "I am a beatnik but not a total nonconformist. I believe in bathing." It comes off as condescending today; Stevens, with his sensitive cultural antennae, probably sensed that then.

But the Prophet became the home base for a trio called JPM—John Sweet, Peter Kolesar and Matthew Knott Johnson. The latter sang leads, and the others provided harmonies, while Sweet played guitar and Kolesar played banjo and guitar. "We were good; we could sing a whole line without taking a breath," says Knott Johnson, now a retired professional caregiver living in Atlanta.

Kolesar had come to Cincinnati in 1959–60 from New York City, where he had completed an undergraduate degree in physics and math at Queens College and worked at Procter & Gamble (P&G). He found housing at an SRO, the L.B. Harrison Club at Victory Parkway and East McMillan Street in Walnut Hills, for young men who were new to the city and on tight budgets. Looking for someone to play music with, Kolesar connected with Sweet and Knott Johnson—both still in high school—and they started practicing together, performing songs rooted in Sweet's interest in folk's leftist political tradition and Kolesar's affinity for traditional American music.

Kolesar also discovered bluegrass while in Cincinnati. Some other L.B. Harrison occupants were southerners who liked to attend a bluegrass club on McMillan Street that was within walking distance. So, Kolesar went with them. Although he doesn't recall the club's name all these decades later, it could have been the Ken Mill Tavern (or Café) at the corner of McMillan and Kenton Streets. "We had a small crew of us guys at L.B. Harrison [who] just loved that stuff," said Kolesar, who went on to earn a doctorate at Columbia and is now a professor emeritus at Columbia University's Graduate School of Business. "You stood there in awe at how good those guys were."

A fulltime bluegrass bar throughout the 1960s, owned by Stu and Ann Salmons, Ken Mill Tavern featured the local band Earl Taylor and the Stoney Mountain Boys and hosted such traveling acts as the Stanley Brothers and Osborne Brothers. (The tavern is the subject of a wonderful remembrance by Chris Smith, an Ohio-based bluegrass musician and festival promoter, as well as a Stanley Brothers historian, on www.bluegrasstoday.com, where I found this information.)

With those mixed influences and plenty of practice, the JPM trio became ambitious. "We thought we were getting pretty good," Kolesar said. "One of us heard about the Prophet, so we just screwed up our courage one night and drove down there, walked in and asked the manager if we could play. We were shocked when he said, 'OK, go up there and show what you got.' It had a basement where we ran through one or two numbers, went up on stage, and he said, 'You're hired.' I don't think he paid us very much, and we passed the hat."

Kolesar questions journalist Stevens's assertion that the Prophet was ersatz. "I don't know about that," he says. "There were regular people and then Beat people. We would play, and people wouldn't applaud but snap their fingers. That was the thing, like you're being cool." He also recalls the venue selling a brochure-size anthology of Beat poetry, such as work by Gregory Corso, and having poetry readings.

The Prophet did hire at least one act that would blow the minds of any unsuspecting squares who wandered in—the hipster-beloved fast-talking comedian Lord Buckley. He did seven nights a week for two weeks— sometimes two shows per night—at the club in July 1960. (The pace may have

The JPM Trio (plus one) at Seven Cities in 1961. *Left to right*: Matthew Knott Johnson, Peter Kolesar, Danny Cox and John Sweet. *Courtesy of Peter Kolesar.*

taken its toll; Buckley died of a stroke at the age of fifty-four in November of that year.) Stevens may have not liked the place, but he liked Buckley. "When he is really rolling along, the lines are spoken in rhythmic chant, though he might change octaves dramatically," he wrote. "Far out? Certainly. Almost too far to understand if you're not of the hip school....He's far out, but he can be reached."

Kolesar went back to Columbia for a master's degree in industrial engineering in 1962 and a doctorate in 1964, but he returned to Cincinnati in the summers of 1962 and 1963 to work at P&G. By then, the Prophet was gone, but he had the chance to play music with his trio and sometimes with an additional member, Cox—he has kept a photograph of the quartet playing at Seven Cities for all these years.

Kolesar also found some interesting gigs aside from Seven Cities. "Through P&G, I hooked into a crew of guys my age starting their careers, and they were the P&G version of *Mad Men*, their advertising guys," he said. "They had a bit of money, and they threw a pretty interesting party somewhere on Mount Adams, and we were entertainment." (This party might have been held at the venerable Blind Lemon, which opened in the spring of 1963, as Kolesar remembers it having indoor and outdoor space.)

Sweet, Cox's early folk-singing partner at Seven Cities, deserves a mention, too. As the *Atlanta Journal-Constitution* related after his death in 2020, he bought four dilapidated homes in a struggling inner-city neighborhood known as Inman Park in 1971, while he was still a law student at Atlanta's Emory University. Recognizing the difficulty of getting home loans for such areas, Sweet and a friend founded one of the country's first community federal credit unions, and, with a law partner, also started buying and rehabbing homes in the neighborhood.

As a lawyer, according to his obituary, Sweet was devoted to workers' compensation claims and did a lot of volunteer and pro bono work. He served one term on Atlanta's city council, and afterward, he remained a political activist whose impact was felt nationally. The obituary stated: "Though he held office only one term, he'd spend much of his remaining life scouting, identifying and coaching a litany of progressive candidates, particularly women and minorities. A partial list of his protégés includes John Lewis, whom he helped get elected to city council. Later would come the likes of State Senator Mary Margaret Oliver, and State Representatives Stephanie Stuckey and Stacey Abrams."

But music—the kind of music Seven Cities offered a showcase for—remained with Sweet. "John loved Seven Cities and Fellowship House and talked about them throughout our life together," said his widow, Midge, via email. To quote the obituary, "A guitarist and singer most of his life, Sweet spent decades compiling music ranging from civil rights songs to Appalachian music, union tunes, protest songs or, as Midge Sweet said, 'the more radical the song, the better.'"

He also, beginning in the late 1990s, had friends come over for Wednesday night hootenannies in his basement. Knott Johnson, who had remained close friends with Sweet in Atlanta, used to come over to join in, and Felson occasionally visited from Athens. It was like a circle unbroken. When asked what those sessions were like, Knott Johnson immediately began to sing "Bob Dylan's Dream" from the 1962 album *The Freewheelin' Bob Dylan*. It was a song, he said, that he and Sweet had been singing together since it was new and had never forgotten. After Cincinnati, both had spent time together in New York in the 1960s, attending Columbia University and experiencing changing times. Knott Johnson choked up a little while singing a couple of verses, including the final one:

> *I wish, I wish, I wish in vain*
> *That we could sit simply in that room again.*
> *Ten thousand dollars at the drop of a hat,*
> *And I'd give it all gladly if our lives could be like that.*

"We sang that throughout our whole life," Knott Johnson said. "It was kind of our anthem for loving and caring for one another in a wider circle from our youth."

In late 1963, Seven Cities became Club Tulu, a teenage key club operated by popular top 40 format WSAI disc jockey Ron Britain (whose on-air phrase was "So long, tulu buddies"). It packed in five hundred kids to see Cincinnati guitar superstar Lonnie Mack. Dorfman did still hold a hootenanny there; around the same time, news reports say he planned for a never-realized major Cincinnati Folk Festival. Britain left for a radio job in Cleveland in early 1964, and then the place became the Varsity Mug Club, which offered live music beginning with the local rock group Them, which featured Buddy Holly devotee Stan Hertzman. Later, the Mug Club's owners bought an old garage space on Ludlow Avenue in Clifton's Gaslight District. But they couldn't get a liquor license and wound up leasing to someone who entertained the radical idea of operating a concert venue without liquor. The business owner was Jim Tarbell, and the place became Ludlow Garage.

But that's another chapter in the story of Cincinnati's lost concert venues.

6

NEIGHBORHOODS AND BEYOND

*O*utside of downtown, thriving venues for live music existed in Cincinnati's inner-city neighborhoods, as well as in the suburbs and beyond. They showcased jazz, rock, country and many other forms of popular music. They also did brisk business in northern Kentucky, as I have written.

Indeed, looking at old newspaper advertisements and stories about these clubs and concert halls, you realize how historically important such (mostly) small venues were for giving artists, now cherished worldwide—from John Coltrane to the Byrds—an early career boost in Cincinnati. Even though the places are now gone, they should live on in memory as hallowed ground.

For instance, a Walnut Hills establishment run by Lucy Green, the New Cotton Club, in November 1962 brought in a young, still-little-known pop-leaning singer named Aretha Franklin. (However, she already had buzz as a budding jazzy stylist. She was supposed to play a month earlier with the Ike & Tina Turner Revue at the huge, but by then fading, concert venue near Roselawn called Castle Farm, but she canceled out. And in October, she got booked onto a revue at Music Hall.)

These clubs also allowed local performers—jazz musicians, like Dee Felice, Lee Stolar, Jimmy McGary and Carmon DeLeone; comedians and singing entertainers, like Clarence Loos and Ronnie Hollyman—to stay busy and sometimes even manage their own clubs. And it allowed disc jockeys, especially at the jazz station WNOP-AM, to be entertainment power brokers.

This book already has presented full separate chapters on two venues—
Surf Club and Seven Cities—that were early responders to the new hip
changes awakening America. And it will have a later chapter on one
neighborhood jazz club, Babe Baker's, which has such an extraordinary
history that it, too, merits a special chapter. But what follows in this chapter
are some stories and anecdotes about specific noteworthy Cincinnati
neighborhood clubs and other venues for live music in the 1950s and 1960s
that now are gone and deserve some recognition. Not all are included—
that would take a book devoted just to them, maybe several. But what
would a Cincinnati "lost venue" history be without mentioning, say, a place
in downtown St. Bernard called Jazz Bohemia, which existed from 1958 to
1961. It was an early local reflector of the Beat culture, and it embraced
seriously contemplative jazz, recitations of modernist poetry and a worldly
coffeehouse atmosphere.

Early on, the West End was a vibrant center for live music, especially
jazz, until the Black neighborhood's size was reduced by urban renewal,
the construction of Interstate 75 and the creation of the Queensgate light
industry area. "I played double bass with the Don Linder Quartet, and

The Regal Theater in the West End, seen here in 1984. *Photograph by David Coyle; courtesy of
the* Cincinnati Enquirer.

we played bars in the West End, like the Playboy Club, the 936 Club, the Cotton Club, etc.," said Roger Abramson via email, who went on to be a busy concert promoter and talent manager in the 1960s. "We also played inner-city school dances, the Lockland Roller Dome and every Sunday night at the Ritz ballroom on Central Avenue, which was the number-one spot at the time, packed with 500 young people. One of my all-time best memories."

There was also one cluster of clubs offering live music, often jazz, in Walnut Hills, spilling over a bit into East Walnut Hills. Aside from the aforementioned New Cotton Club, there were the Diplomat Club, Mother's, the Rainbow Club, Herbie's Neoteric Jazz Lounge and the Key Room. The latter is immortalized in the King Records album *Shhh! The Quiet Man Ronny Hollyman Recorded Live at the Exclusive Key Room.*

Farther out on Eastern Avenue was Vet's Inn, where Cincinnati blues star Albert Washington played. Over in the West End, proprietor Marie Byndon brought top jazz acts to the Misty Lounge. Over-the-Rhine had its country music scene that flowered in the 1970s with Aunt Maudie's on Main Street. Over-the-Rhine was also home to the Swing Bar at Thirteenth and Vine Streets, which promised "red-hot live music, dancing, go-go girls [and] surprises galore." It could reportedly get as wild as one of the acts that played there, Hoppin' Harry & the Wild Ones. *Cincinnati Post* columnist Tom Murphy remembered it in 1978 as "an open invitation to trouble."

Clubs with live entertainment were scattered along or near Reading Road from just north of what is now Martin Luther King Jr. Drive through Roselawn to the Reading border. Among them were the Cabana Lounge (with soulful R&B acts like Big Maybelle and H-Bomb Ferguson, as well as jazz guitarist Wes Montgomery), Cock & Bull, the Whisper Room, Buccaneer Inn, Danny's Jubilee Lounge, Stein's Hideaway and the drink spots at the modernist Carousel Inn in Roselawn.

The Top Shelf, right at Reading Road and Rockdale Avenue in Avondale's heart, was initially a key club that once humorously apologized in print to its headliner, the blind jazz multi-instrumentalist Roland Kirk, for the small size of its newspaper advertisement promoting his engagement. It also had some top-shelf acts, like singers Betty Carter and Johnny Hartman. In 1966, the Living Room's Mel Herman and his brother Jerry took over the club and changed its name to Baby Grand. They offered jazz organist Brother Jack McDuff as the opening act. A year later, Babe Baker took it over from them and eventually changed the name to Mr. B's. It had go-go girls in the late 1960s.

Even the far northern reaches of the greater Cincinnati area played a role in introducing patrons to the changing music of the 1960s. At Spatz Show Bar in Hamilton, an act playing two shows on March 3, 1961, was advertised as the Miracles and "The Shop Around Boys" to connect the group with its hit 1960 song, "Shop Around." Not advertised was that the Miracles featured Smokey Robinson as their lead singer or that they were part of Detroit's then-new Motown Records—it was too early for either name to have much general recognition. Out by Colerain Avenue and Springdale Road in the northern reaches of Hamilton County, Club Touchez featured "swinging rock," twist and limbo contests and, in 1962, presented another rising Motown act, the Contours ("Do You Love Me"). And a bit north of Hamilton, on U.S. Route 127, was the Dude Ranch, where "recording and movie star" Jerry Lee Lewis and his trio appeared for three shows per night—with the last starting at 1:30 a.m.—on three May nights in 1961 and then came roaring back for more in February 1962.

Meanwhile, LeSourdsville Lake Amusement Park, already four decades old, began undergoing a youthful transformation to welcome in the 1960s. In 1961, Howard Berni and Frank Murru purchased it from its original owner, Edgar Streifthau. (According to Scott Fowler's Images of America book about the venue, as well as the *Cincinnati Post*, sales manager George "Bill" Barr bought out Murru in 1964.) Because of the park's Stardust Gardens Ballroom, the new management chose a live entertainment strategy that would appeal to rock 'n' roll–loving adolescent boomers.

In 1962, *American Bandstand*'s Dick Clark appeared with several regional acts either aiming for national success or already enjoying it—Dale Wright and the Wright Guys, Teddy and the Roughriders, Carl Dobkins Jr. and the Casinos. The Beach Boys arrived in August 1963, not long after their breakthrough "Surfin' U.S.A." topped the charts and made surfing a national craze. When the Byrds visited in July 1965, they were a new and super-hot top 40 act whose smash-hit version of Bob Dylan's "Mr. Tambourine Man" had launched the folk-rock genre. In 1976, under general manager Bill Robinson, the park once again got a boost from rock—WSAI-AM started sponsoring Rock 'N Remember shows with such top names from the past as Bobby Lewis, Danny & the Juniors, Herman's Hermits and Tommy James and the Shondells. The venue's name changed to Americana Amusement Park in 1977, which lasted until the place closed in 1999. (There was a brief attempt to reopen in 2002.)

Live music events could also occur at offbeat locations. Joey Dee, the creator of the "Peppermint Twist," appeared at Bond Hill's Twin Drive-

Bond Hill's Swifton Center hosted an outdoor show by Blues Magoos in 1967. *Photograph by Stu Levy.*

In and at Swifton Shopping Center, the postwar modernist gem that was demolished in the 2010s. The psychedelic pop act Blues Magoos ("We Ain't Got Nothin' Yet") also did a Swifton promotion in 1967, as well as an appearance at the old Western Woods Mall on the city's far west side. The Regal and State, two West End movie theaters appealing to Black audiences, had the occasional live show as well—the Regal brought in Harlem Capers of 1963, featuring "a stage full of big stars," plus the Valiants, and at the end of 1956, it booked King Records star Tiny Bradshaw ("Train Kept a Rollin'") and his orchestra for three shows.

Some special appearances seem strange today. In January 1964, a movie theater in Norwood called Fine Arts Plaza announced that Dave Mathews's group would play jazz and then George Thompson would do a narrative about the biblical figure Job to celebrate the opening of Luis Buñuel's Spanish art film *Viridiana*. Whoever planned that presentation on Job—who is tormented by an angel named Satan after God refuses to protect him—knew what they were doing. *Viridiana* is a dark satire of religion by the atheist Buñuel that focuses on the disillusionment of a nun amid much debauchery around her. But however appropriate, it's a film that hardly needs warm-up entertainment.

One club that hosted an occasional titan of soul and blues music yet is barely remembered today was Club Ramon, at 282 Stark Street in Over-the-Rhine, just off Central Parkway. The club got several mentions in newspapers from 1962 to 1967—mostly small advertisements for its talent shows, limbo contests and local acts, as well as its classified advertisements for waitresses. But for the Cincinnati-born musician Danny Adler, a teenage guitar prodigy who went on to front a popular roots-oriented British band called the Roogalators in the 1970s ("Cincinnati Fatback"), Club Ramon provided a life-changing experience. Adler started playing in Cincinnati blues, soul and rock clubs in the 1960s. "In 1967, my cousin came from New York to visit, and I said Slim Harpo was playing in a club near downtown," he told me during an interview for a 2015 *Cincinnati Enquirer* story. (I did not use this anecdote then.)

Harpo, a Louisiana-born blues singer, harmonica player and guitarist beloved by the Rolling Stones, ZZ Top and other rock bands, had such now-classic 1960s hits as "Baby Scratch My Back," "I'm a King Bee" and "Rainin' in My Heart." He favored an atmospheric, laid-back style called "swamp blues." Adler said:

> We went to Club Ramon early, and there's Slim Harpo eating dinner and playing cards. I said, "Mr. Harpo, I know your real name is James Moore, so what should I call you?" He said, "You can call me Slim." I said, "I have a band, and we do some of your songs." He said, "What do you play?" And I said, "Guitar." He took me back to the dressing room and put on me a beautiful Gibson 330 [electric guitar] with black plastic pick-ups and said, "Let me hear what you do."

Adler played guitar in B.B. King's fluid style.

> He [Harpo] said, "Wow, that's out of sight. I want you to play with me tonight." I was stunned. He said, "I was going to pay you, 25 cents," which was actually $25, good money in 1967. I said I wasn't worried about money. I was just blown away he wanted me.
>
> They didn't have a house band at Club Ramon. It was a Hammond B3 (organ) and a drummer—no bass player because the Hammond player kicked bass pedals. So, Harpo would have had to play his own guitar.

The bluesman told Adler, "'This way, I can play harmonica and do my stage moves and I know you'll have guitar covered.' We hit the stage at [9:00 p.m.], and it was beautiful."

One of the hotter clubs for rock in the early 1960s was Hawaiian Gardens in Western Hills at 6289 Glenway Avenue. This was where Lonnie Mack, one of the greatest rock guitarists that the greater Cincinnati area ever produced (he was from nearby West Harrison, Indiana) played when he was issuing the unforgettable hit songs "Memphis" and "Wham" with their scorching instrumentals.

The *Post*'s Stevens went to see Mack and band at Hawaiian Gardens in late December 1963, when they were playing a series of gigs through New Year's Eve. "I went out among them last night," he reported. "There with the bouffant hairdos outnumbering the ponytails about 134 to nothing, I watched the young set dancing 'The Dog' and listening to Lonnie's amazing guitar....He is a country boy who plays and sings Negro blues, spacing it with gospel screams and shouts. His guitar technique is complex and rhythmic, with a deep subconscious feeling for jazz as expressed through the blues."

The Inner Circle Nightclub at 2621 Vine Street in Corryville, near the University of Cincinnati, was one of the higher-profile and more successful live music venues while it lasted, from 1965 to 1975, but it is obscure now because of what replaced it—the celebrated rock club Bogart's, which is still in business as of this writing, although it had been inactive throughout the COVID-19 pandemic. The building had been the Nordland Movie Theater for decades, and in its last years as a theater, it was managed by entrepreneurs who experimented with silent movies (along with a live pianist and magician) and serious art films, such as *The Rest Is Silence*, a drama about post–World War II Germany based on *Hamlet*.

When Inner Circle opened in August 1965, it was as a six-hundred-person "plush cocktail lounge with entertainment," according to the *Post*, and it featured local singer Judy James with accompanying jazz musicians. However, it seemed to find its stride booking veteran rock and soul acts, sometimes with their top 40 success behind them—Joey Dee, Little Eva (of "Locomotion" fame), the Platters, Little Richard—as well as hardworking contemporary R&B singers, like Joe Simon. One heavily promoted attraction was the fourteen-piece show band Wayne Cochran and the C.C. Riders, which Inner Circle called the "best known act in the country." With his white-haired pompadour, dynamically vigorous voice and a stage presence that fans considered to be as energetic as James Brown's, Cochran was a live show phenomenon who never had any big hits.

King Records scholars have done much research on how Inner Circle's house band, the Cincinnati Kids, came to the attention of James Brown, the superstar of Cincinnati's King Records label. He started to use them—

under the name the Dapps—along with their friend drummer/singer Beau Dollar (William Bowman, who had played with Lonnie Mack and the Coins) on recordings. Extensive information about the connections between these musicians can be found in a lengthy and informative 2020 posting titled "The Dapps at King Records" on Chris Richardson's fascinating blog at www.zeroto180.org, which features his own research, as well as that of Randy McNutt and Brian Powers, among others.

Less celebrated today is another would-be Inner Circle–inspired divine pairing, Cincinnati Reds superstar catcher Johnny Bench and a show band called Mickey-Larry and the Exciters. After Bench, a country music fan, joined Mickey-Larry for some November 1970 performances, they announced plans for an album to be released the following March called *Johnny Bench, Mickey-Larry and the Exciters Live at Inner Circle*, featuring versions of such hit songs as "Fire and Rain" and "By the Time I Get to Phoenix." (A fan who wrote to the *Enquirer* also mentioned "Share the Land," the Guess Who's 1970 hit that was criticized for being "socialist.") It was subsequently reported that Bench still had recording plans, but that was it.

As is common near universities nationwide, the commercial streets closest to the University of Cincinnati (UC) were home to many bars and clubs with live entertainment. In the 1960s, when Ohio allowed the consumption of 3.2-proof beer by those who were eighteen and older—as boomers were reaching that age—the immediate off-campus area was quite lively. I've mentioned the Mug Club previously, but there were also places like the Pickle Barrel, Round Table, Golden Door, jazz musician Ed Moss's Love's Coffee House and the brilliant guitarist Sandy Nassan's acoustic-oriented Family Owl at the Candlelight. If you want to know what that overall scene was like, you can hear a 1966 rehearsal tape from the excellent Cincinnati garage band Dauphine St./Street Blues at www.dsblues.com/vintage.

The celebrated singer David Pomeranz, who has also had a successful career as a composer—his work has been covered by Barry Manilow ("Tryin' to Get That Feeling Again" and "The Old Songs"), Bette Midler, the Carpenters and many others—played at the Pickle Barrel as a member of East Orange Express and elsewhere as a solo act. A native of Long Island, Pomeranz came to Cincinnati in 1968. "We played Pickle Barrel (at 2507 West Clifton Avenue) something like once a week for six months or a year or something," Pomeranz said in a phone interview, then continued:

> *We just played a lot at that club. My recollection is it had wooden chairs*
> *and tables; I don't remember a place to dance. I remember very well the*

bandstand and the songs we did—the Vanilla Fudge version of "You Keep Me Hangin' On," Spirit's "I Got a Line on You, Babe"—and we did a couple of originals. We had a Hammond B-3 Organ like Vanilla Fudge or the Young Rascals did with a growling great sound.

He also remembered that the group did a show-stopping, crowd-pleasing version of "Leaving on a Jet Plane," with him taking lead (you can hear it on YouTube).

Pomeranz studied philosophy at UC but spent most of his time making music. He was lead singer for East Orange Express in 1968–69 and then a local solo performer until he signed with Decca Records and went to New York to record in 1970. (Two albums for the label, *New Blues* and *Time to Fly*, came out in 1971.) Before he left Cincinnati, Pomeranz also played at the Family Owl inside the Candlelight at 277 Calhoun Street. The Family Owl's guiding light, Nassan, released his own album, *Just Guitar*, in 1970 on jazz star Herbie Mann's Embryo label. "Those days were exciting because a lot of invention was going on there—he had a very inventive approach to playing guitar," Pomeranz said. "And there was just this little group of interesting musicians there, and I was thrilled to be part of it. I'm kind of known for doing pop, but we got into improvisational jazz. I played piano, guitar and drums."

East Orange Express, meanwhile, did all right without Pomeranz—three of its members, bassist Mike Reilly, keyboardist Mike Connor and drummer Billy Hinds went on to perform with Pure Prairie League.

Within Cincinnati's Black community, Avondale's Wein Bar was a place with a storied history and an important role in Cincinnati's civil rights movement. The Wein Bar also featured live music—at least occasionally. Proprietor Abraham "Abe" K. Goldhagen's place was located at Rockdale Avenue and Reading Road from 1957 to 1970 and then moved a block away for its remaining decade in business. It closed when Goldhagen retired in 1980. But the club's roots extend back to 1934.

A Jewish man, Goldhagen was the oldest of nine children. According to a 1981 *Cincinnati Enquirer* article, he grew up in the poorer neighborhoods of Toledo, Detroit, Boston and Cincinnati. Goldhagen was also the longtime treasurer for the local NAACP. "If you went to the Wein Bar on Rockdale, he'd always serve you a drink and find out if you had a NAACP membership," said Hasker Nelson, a now retired community affairs director of WCPO-TV and producer/host of its *Black Memo* program. Nelson has researched Cincinnati's Black history.

Abe Goldhagen outside of his last Wein Bar in Avondale, 1980. *Photograph by Mark Treitel; courtesy of the* Cincinnati Enquirer.

When Goldhagen retired, he looked back in a 1980 feature by the *Enquirer*'s Allen Howard, a Black reporter with a deep knowledge of the importance of the city's institutions serving the Black community. The Wein Bar (sometimes referred to as the Wein-Bar) was founded in 1934, when relatives Bernie Weinstein and Isadora Barnett opened a café in the West End. This was during the Great Depression, and Goldhagen, his father, Joseph, and other family members got a liquor license and joined in. They moved the establishment to 413 West Sixth Street on the eastern fringes of the West End in 1936. The bar moved to Walnut Hills in 1937, around the same time that the family sold another business they owned, Downtown's Kipp's Café, because the city wouldn't let them serve Black people. In 1938, the Walnut Hills site was advertising "the hottest colored band in town," with two complete floor shows nightly, plus door prizes.

In 1957, Goldhagen moved to Avondale, taking over a place called the 19th Hole Café and renaming it. Avondale, traditionally a Jewish neighborhood, was seeing a growth in its Black population, as plans were afoot to demolish portions of the West End to make way for urban renewal and an expressway. "I guess the Wein Bar pretty much became the unofficial NAACP office," Goldhagen told Howard in 1980. "We would have four or five NAACP benefit shows a year. I remember we were able to raise enough money through benefit shows to send 50 people to the Freedom March in Washington, D.C., in August of 1963." In a 1981 article, also written by Howard, Goldhagen proudly said, "The group that went to Selma, Alabama, for a freedom march in [1965] gathered at the bar the night before."

But music played a role in Wein Bar history, too. Nancy Goldhagen's late husband, Michael, Abe's nephew, worked at the Wein Bar. "My husband used to talk about the Black artists that played at the bar before they became so famous. Bootsy Collins was one," she said via email. It's conceivable that William "Bootsy" Collins, the Rock & Roll Hall of Fame bassist so associated with funk music, was playing a fundraiser at the Wein Bar on March 8, 1970, the day his big break came. Bobby Byrd, an emissary of James Brown, called for Collins and his band the Pacemakers (which included Collins's brother Phelps, or "Catfish," on rhythm guitar) to come to Columbus, Georgia, to work for Brown. Bootsy subsequently wound up changing popular music as a member of Brown's band, the J.B.'s, and then P-Funk and Bootsy's Rubber Band.

But it's hard to firmly establish that the Wein Bar in Avondale is where this serendipitous summoning occurred. The Wein Bar held benefit events with music on Sundays, the night the call would have happened, but I couldn't find a newspaper notice of an event with the Pacemakers for the date in question. And while the momentous (in hindsight) occurrence has gotten plenty of coverage in the music press, print accounts of the event have referred to the site as "the Wine Bar" or "a wine bar," as well as a "Wine Bar on Gilbert Avenue" in Walnut Hills.

The closest thing to confirmation came in an online account on www.wattpad.com from Destiny Hogue's book *Tales from the Tour Bus: The Vickery Family*. It features an oral history–style interview with Bootsy Collins and Pacemakers drummer Frank "Kash" Waddy. Here's the excerpt:

> *Frankie: One night, we played at this place called the Wein Bar, on the corner of Rockdale and Redding [sic] Road. We made $14 total.*

Bootsy: So, we were playing, jamming on stage, you know. Next thing I know, the bartender came up and said, "Bobby Byrd is on the phone."

Unfortunately, despite repeated attempts, neither Bootsy nor Waddy could be reached to clarify these events for this book.

Before he retired, Goldhagen faced some tough days at the Wein Bar, as drugs and crime made the early 1970s an edgy time in Cincinnati. In 1970, he was robbed while returning from the bank. And in 1972, a man under the influence of drugs who had been seen at the bar shot and killed the male companion with whom Goldhagen and a woman were walking. Abe Goldhagen died in 1992 at the age of eighty-seven. "I not only lost a friend but one of the hardest workers for justice I have ever known," said Frank Allison, the local NAACP president, at the news of Goldhagen's death. And Cincinnati lost an important citizen.

7

BABE BAKER'S

*A*mid the wealth of neighborhood music clubs in the 1950s and 1960s, one really stands out—Babe Baker's Jazz Corner at 3128 Reading Road in Avondale. In fact, this was perhaps the city's most important jazz club of its time, from its inception in 1958 as a venue booking major acts until it petered out in the late 1960s. (Even during that time, there were periods when Edward "Babe" Baker suspended the format.)

The acts Baker brought in—Lester Young, Cannonball Adderley, Hank Mobley, Kenny Durham, Ben Webster, Lou Donaldson and the Pierce-Plum Quartet (whose members recorded with Cincinnati-born composer/pianist George Russell)—mattered then and now. An especially stand-out act was the performer who was booked for the first week of 1963—the fiery, revolutionary tenor (and sometimes soprano) saxophonist John Coltrane and his classic quartet, featuring drummer Elvin Jones, pianist McCoy Tyner and bassist Jimmy Garrison. Coltrane, as a band leader, only played in Cincinnati one other time after this intimate club engagement—that was when his classic quartet had top billing at the Ohio Valley Jazz Festival in 1965. He died at the age of forty in 1967.

I think the site where Babe Baker's was located should have a historical marker honoring this engagement—it was that monumental. But don't take my word for it. *Cincinnati Post* entertainment editor and writer Dale Stevens wrote upon his retirement in 1988 that the by-then-long-gone venue was "a great jazz room" and rhapsodized about its presentation of Coltrane as "the single greatest (Cincinnati) attraction ever." And when jazz radio station WNOP tried to start a Cincinnati Jazz Hall of Fame in 1983, Baker, because of his jazz club, was among the first group nominated for inclusion. (He was not inducted that year.) Even as late as 1996, Coltrane's appearance at Baker's was singled out by the *Enquirer*'s Larry Nager as one key event in establishing that "Cincinnati was a stop on the road to greatness for some top names in jazz and R&B."

Baker was a well-known figure both within the Black community and, at least to music lovers, outside of it as well. He merited a Stevens profile in the *Post* back in 1963, because he "has presented more music in his nightclubs than any other entrepreneur. He owns five taverns, plus part-ownership in a sixth, and once owned nine. He is best known for the club that bears his name, where he has presented many of the important performers in the jazz field."

Baker also shared with Stevens some of his early experiences in the Cincinnati jazz life, such as managing a Walnut Hills club called Duffy's Tavern when the jazz group consisted of future stars Billy Mitchell, Art Blakey and Tadd Dameron, but their pay was just twenty-five dollars per week.

In the profile, Stevens detailed Baker's life. His nickname, Babe, came from being a homerun hitter in sandlot baseball. He moved to Cincinnati from West Virginia, where his father was a coal miner. He quit school at age twelve, in seventh grade, and he worked as a dishwasher until he was able to buy his first club at the age of twenty-eight. Baker was also a popular WSAI-AM disc jockey for several years, beginning in 1951; he staged benefit shows and, in general, made a name for himself. As a disc jockey, he had an evening show called *Harlem Express* that, according to *Post* radio listings, "takes off for another trip through Rhythm Land." In 1954, Baker and WNOP's Ernie Waits were both named among the country's leading radio deejays by *Color Magazine*—giving Cincinnati two of the ten spots in this Black publication's poll.

At the time of the 1963 Stevens interview, Baker had held a real estate license for a year and was considering leaving the nightclub business. "There's a small pool of good talent with drawing capacity, and you have to pay them so high, they earn all the profits," Baker told Stevens. "I'd rather have just a saloon any day."

There may be a bit more to Baker's story than that. Hasker Nelson, who has researched Cincinnati's Black community, got to know an elderly Baker in the early 2000s. They would have breakfast at the Sugar n' Spice restaurant on Reading Road in Paddock Hills, Nelson recalled. With encouragement, Baker told his story to Nelson and provided some photographs and mementoes. This history is extremely useful now, because when Baker died in 2005 at the age of eighty-nine, there wasn't much fanfare. The obituary listed no survivors. His wife, sister and brother were deceased, and he had requested no services.

"I started from his very beginnings, when he was a kid down in West End," Nelson said in an interview about his talks with Baker:

> *He was really dirt poor. He worked at the Cotton Club for a guy by the name of Henry Ferguson. And that's the guy he credits for getting him into the business frame of mind. So, he learned the ropes about the bar and club business from him.*
>
> *He worked at the Cotton Club as a janitor and was promoted to bartender. He also drove a Ferguson cab—Mr. Ferguson owned a cab company, a Black equivalent of Yellow Cab. Mr. Ferguson actually got cabs from Yellow Cab and put "Ferguson Cabs" on it.*
>
> *Babe drove cabs after he got off work at Cotton Club; he'd go home and get a wink or two of sleep and come back to the club.*

Cincinnati's Cotton Club, itself named after the club in Harlem, used the ballroom at the Hotel Sterling, at the corner of Sixth and Mound Streets in the West End, to present the finest jazz players and singers, along with floor shows, to a Cincinnati audience for some thirty years. The club started to struggle in the 1950s and was bought by the city for "urban renewal" in 1960. As historian Cissy Hill recounted in a *Cincinnati Enquirer* story from 1981, Ferguson had leased the business from the hotel owner and ran it— opting to sublease it—until his death. When he died in 1946 of a heart attack, the *Cincinnati Post* listed as his numerous assets a majority ownership in Babe Baker Inc. restaurants.)

Ferguson's widow, Lulu Belle, then attempted to keep it going—at one point getting economic help from Ezzard Charles, the heavyweight champion boxer known as the Cincinnati Cobra. With different management, the club finally moved to Walnut Hills at 966 East McMillan Street before closing. (Later, there was briefly a New Cotton Club in Walnut Hills.)

Baker ran a tavern before Babe Baker's Jazz Club—there is a photograph of him stylishly dressed in an argyle sweater in a broadcast booth inside what appears to be such a place. Nelson says the photograph is of Baker at his Log Cabin Inn, located in the West End. Katherine Gartrell, whose sister was married to Ezzard Charles, recalled seeing Baker broadcast from the Log Cabin Inn.

In early 1958, *Cincinnati Enquirer* writer Arthur Darack visited Babe Baker's Jazz Corner and discovered it was something new and special. He had been invited as part of a press/fan tour to hear the New Jazz Disciples, a local group that played at Baker's and was getting a major push. Managed by WNOP disc jockey and jazz buff Dick Pike, the Disciples played at Babe Baker's often. "The room was quiet; the mood was that of a concert where food and drink were available," Darack wrote. "Since jazz is one of the most esoteric of art forms, Baker's Cocktail Lounge seemed the other night like something far removed from the usual nightclub."

Based on a photograph provided by Nelson, as well as his description, Babe Baker's Jazz Corner was a compact place—the front door was in the middle of one side; inside, the room had a small horizontal front window and then tables for two along a partly-cushioned wall, each with an ashtray. Above the padding was eye-catching wallpaper with a piano keyboard motif. "It was only one room wide," Nelson said. "Babe put a mirror up behind the bar and on the other side of the room from the bar was the bandstand. Because of the mirror, it looked bigger than it was."

Melvin Grier, a retired *Cincinnati Post* photographer, was still underage when he and his father moved from the West End to Burnet Avenue, near Erkenbrecher Avenue in Avondale around 1959 or 1960. "I was in easy walking distance of Babe Baker's," he said:

> The first time I went over there and took a seat, the waitress—in those days, we still called them that instead of waiters or servers—came over and looked at me and said, "Now, baby, you're too young to be in here. You'll have to come back for the matinee." I left and did come back that Sunday. It was (organist) Shirley Scott with (saxophonist) Eddie "Lockjaw" Davis, and the club had a really great atmosphere. A fair amount of people were in there for a Sunday afternoon. It was not large at all, but it's the music that makes the club, not the club that makes the music.

The famous—calling it "legendary" would not be hyperbole—Coltrane engagement occurred from January 7 to January 13, 1963. It was recognized as a big deal at the time. An advertisement called Coltrane "the nation's most talked-about saxophonist," and *Enquirer* columnist Luke Feck touted the upcoming shows of the "furious fire-hot saxophonist." Coltrane was just thirty-six when he played this gig, but he had built an extraordinary reputation since leaving Miles Davis's group in 1960, where he had attracted praise for his "sheets of sound" style of playing tenor saxophone. (On

February 5, 1959, Coltrane was with Davis's sextet at Newport's Copa Club.) As a leader of his own group, his albums like *Giant Steps* and *My Favorite Things* (on which he played soprano sax) were winning praise. For this show, Coltrane appeared not only with his "classic quartet" but also with Eric Dolphy—who had played with Coltrane earlier—on bass clarinet, flute and alto saxophone.

Lou Lausche, a then-young jazz bassist and law student, remembered seeing Coltrane on a Saturday night, having chosen him over the virtuoso classical guitarist Andre Segovia, who was performing with the Cincinnati Symphony Orchestra. "It was very much a packed house," he said. "The music was overwhelming; I wasn't expecting it. I was expecting more stuff like what Coltrane did in the 1950s, more melodic. It was all just like screaming, far-out playing. I have to admit I didn't really quite get it. I still don't think it's a very appealing music genre, but John Coltrane certainly had a right to develop his art beyond whatever extent I was able to understand."

Even Babe Baker didn't get it. In Stevens's *Post* review of a show, the journalist and jazz aficionado began his article by describing how a perplexed Baker came up to him and asked, "Explain this to me." Stevens then did so in some of his finest writing I came across while working on this book:

> *Last night I heard Coltrane and his men play only one song. It was "My Favorite Things" and it lasted for 35 minutes. During those 35 minutes, it was organized mayhem that comprised a magnificent jazz chapter....The essence of their approach is virtually complete freedom for each musician. I don't mean to compare their music to a circus, but a good simile is that, like a three-ring circus, you can catch five separate things going on within the Coltrane quartet.*
>
> *As one catches fire, four others flame, too. In one spot, drummer Elvin Jones went into double time for what must have been six or eight minutes. What results are great mountains and valleys of powerful and soft emotion: thoughts and feelings communicated with facile technique in remolding the horizontal shape of the song by exploring the vertical.*

Stevens reached his own beatific epiphany with this statement: "Frankly, I was moved as much as I've ever been shoved around by jazz. Naturally, I didn't fully understand it."

A couple days later, after the group had left town, Stevens published a very touching postscript. Baker had told him that Coltrane had bought forty dollars' worth of vitamins while in town so that he and his men could have the high energy they needed to play at such sustained levels. "But the thing that really amazed Babe was that Trane would go into Babe's office between sets and just sit, with head in hand, thinking about his music," Stevens wrote.

Gartrell, Ezzard Charles's sister-in-law, became friends with both Baker and his wife, Marion, in the 1950s, when Gartrell was a young woman developing a love for jazz and Cincinnati nightlife. (She was born in 1935.) "He was like a father to me," she recalled during a phone interview. She stayed friends with Baker after moving away and would see him occasionally during visits to Cincinnati. Once, Gartrell remembered, she gingerly brought up the subject of last wishes as he was getting older. "I would tease him with, 'What would you like if something happened,'" she explained. "He said, 'I don't want anybody looking down at me. Just let me go.'"

8
I'M SO YOUNG

*W*hile it's important to chronicle the specific venues in Cincinnati's neighborhoods, there was also a greater cultural ecosystem in place that supported live music. This was probably especially important in the Black neighborhoods of the 1950s, since still-rampant segregation limited opportunities elsewhere. In the days before development and divisive expressways chopped up these areas, they were abuzz with enthusiasm for their musicians.

In fact, this ecosystem helped create maybe the greatest (and most timeless) youth-oriented hit to come out of Cincinnati, "I'm So Young" by the Students, a vocal harmony ballad about love thwarted by its narrator's youth. The song's writer, William H. "Prez" Tyus, was himself a student at Cincinnati's old Central High School, a public school known for its vocational curriculum, located on Central Parkway, where Cincinnati State is located now.

Tyus's father owned a West End restaurant, the Buckeye Chili Parlor at 632 Freeman Avenue. "It was the eating place for most of the Black entertainers and sports stars that came through," said Tyus in a phone interview with me from his New York home. "It had collard greens and barbeque ribs, draft beer. We were famous for chili. It was better than all that came later." One of the stars who ate there was tenor saxophone great Lester Young, who played in Cincinnati often in the 1950s on all-star revue lineups or at Babe Baker's club. (Young died in 1959.) The musician was known as "Pres" or "Prez," short for the "president of jazz."

At the same time that Young ate at the family restaurant, Tyus was a gifted writer for Central's school newspaper. "The editor of the school paper was a jazz fan, and when I told him Mr. Young had come into the restaurant, he was fascinated," Tyus explained. "And that's how the name 'Prez' as my nickname evolved." Meanwhile, in one class, Tyus sat behind a "beautiful, beautiful college girl" named—he still vividly remembered—Patricia Pearson. "I sat behind her, and we talked and talked. I liked her, and she liked me, and I was just thinking, and those words came to mind."

In yet another example of that cultural ecosystem, a custodian at Central named Roosevelt Lee was interested in both songwriting and recording. He helped Tyus meet some other music lovers within the Cincinnati Public School System—a Black group known as the D'Italians. Through Lee's connection with record distributor Mel Herman, the ballad was released regionally on the Indianapolis label Note Records (owned by Herman's brother) in 1958. The flip side was another Tyus composition, "Every Day of the Week."

Propelled by singer Leroy King's majestic high voice, "I'm So Young" became a regional favorite. Chicago's Chess Records then released it nationally on different subsidiary labels three times between 1958 and 1964. By doing so, it made the song an enduring classic of the rock musical style known as doo-wop. Since then, "I'm So Young" has been covered by the Ronettes, a solo Ronnie Spector, the Beach Boys, the Del-Vikings, Antony and the Johnsons and others. (A detailed account of the song's recorded history can be found at www.uncamarvy.com.)

In the 1989 book *The Heart of Rock & Soul: The 1001 Greatest Singles Ever Made*, Tyus's and the Students' song made the list at position 254. But the author also interpreted the lyrics to contain a "concluding threat of suicide over being denied the right to marry." That prompted a letter from Tyus to a newspaper denying it, saying its point of view was that of a teenage boy leaving the girl he loves behind to join the navy. "You know what my greatest regret is?" Tyus asked me in our interview. "I never got to tell her [Patricia Pearson] I wrote the song about her. When your book is published, put on a little notation to look for her." So, here it is.

9

THE BEATLES IN CINCINNATI

*O*ne of the more fascinating artifacts of the Beatles' 1964 visit to Cincinnati is a short film clip included in the two-disc DVD *On Tour with the Beatles from LA to Philadelphia.* The telling sequence begins with a shot of the marquee at Cincinnati Gardens, the now-lost municipal arena that opened in 1949 to host hockey and other sporting events, concerts and other programs. Centered on a wide, white plastic backdrop, black capital letters spell out "Beatles Tonite Sold Out." High above, on the otherwise unadorned pinkish brick façade, are the larger white letters designating "Cincinnati Gardens." It's a lonely, ghostly shot, presumably taken soon after the August 27 concert was finished. The scene continues inside, the camera moving through the rows of folding chairs on the arena's floor, a surface littered with debris left by fans. A worker lifting and stacking chairs can be briefly seen. The camera goes in for a close-up of the floor below one seat, and you can see several flashbulbs and a circular decal that says "Thanks WSAI Good Guys for the Beatles" and "Thanks Beatles for Coming!" As another British Invasion band, the Rolling Stones, sang in 1964, "It's All Over Now."

The Beatles' concert on August 27, 1964, took place during the Fab Four's first true North American tour, though they had played two concerts, in New York and Washington, D.C., during their brief February visit to appear on *The Ed Sullivan Show.* The Beatles visited twenty-four cities during August and September 1964. This was the height of Beatlemania, and it was arguably the most talked-about single event ever at the Gardens—the closest competition might have been when Cincinnati Royals guard Adrian Smith scored twenty-four points in twenty-six minutes to be named MVP at the National Basketball Association's 1966 All-Star Game.

The concert elicited massive media coverage when it happened, and it has continued to be the subject of attention—often tied to anniversaries—in newspapers, books, radio broadcasts and social media posts. You can see snippets of the actual performance and the frenetic, ecstatic crowd's response to the group's twenty-eight-minute set on that aforementioned DVD. There is one scene labeled "true sound" of the band playing "She Loves You," and it confirms everything anyone who was there has ever said about the noise level.

The Fab Four's set featured "Twist and Shout" (first made famous, although not originated, by Cincinnati's Isley Brothers), "You Can't Do That," "All My Loving," "She Loves You," "Things We Said Today," Chuck Berry's "Roll Over Beethoven," "Can't Buy Me Love," "If I Fell," "I Want to Hold Your Hand," the Shirelles' "Boys," "A Hard Day's Night" and Little Richard's "Long Tall Sally." The Beatles went on stage after the opening acts at 9:35 p.m., and by 10:10 p.m., they were en route to their waiting plane at Lunken Airport, bound for New York, according to Scott "Belmo" Belmer's *The Beatles Invade Cincinnati 1964 & '66*.

WSAI, the powerhouse top 40 station at 1360 on the AM dial, had been all in on the Beatles since "I Want to Hold Your Hand," their debut single on Capitol Records, was released December 26, 1963. As the British "moptops" and their brightly rocking and youthfully modern "Merseybeat" sound quickly gripped the United States, WSAI did more than just play every Beatles record released. The station's evening deejay, Dusty Rhodes, founded "Dusty Rhodes' Beatle Boosters, North America's First Beatles Fan Club." It grew to twenty-five thousand members, he said.

With that kind of listener response, five WSAI "Good Guys" deejays—Rhodes, Steve Kirk, Paul Purtan, Mark Edwards and "Skinny" Bobby Harper—put up $5,000 each to bring the Beatles to the Gardens during the band's first American tour. When that was announced in April, so many ticket requests came in so quickly that not only were the fourteen thousand seats sold out, but some $30,000 in requests had to be returned. The Good Guys hired Dino Santangelo, the coproducer of the Ohio Valley Jazz Festival and an acquaintance of Purtan's, to produce the event.

The Beatles were a hit machine in April 1964, when the Cincinnati concert was announced. In the first four months of the year, they had had seven top-ten songs, with four reaching no. 1 nationally. They'd also captivated kids across the nation with their *Ed Sullivan Show* appearances, where the televised footage of young girls in the audience screaming became an image inexorably linked to the Beatles' invasion of America.

For some girls at the August Cincinnati Gardens show (and existing footage shows that the audience contained many girls), the event was a veritable pilgrimage. Lindy Kuntz (now Lindy Ranz), an eighth-grader from Harrison, went with girlfriends Pam Viel, Connie White and Bev Pies; Lindy's younger sister, Jody; and Pam's older brother, Terry, who drove. Terry took a picture of them in front of the "Beatles Tonite Sold Out" sign before they all ventured inside. It's daylight outside in the photograph, but there's another reason you can tell it was taken before the show. "We don't look too haggard," Ranz said. That wouldn't have been the case with an "after" photograph. "I know my one friend Bev said, 'I'm not going to scream, I'm not going to scream.' As soon as they came out, that's all you heard was her screaming." And she wasn't the only one. "You couldn't hear a word they were singing," Ranz recalled. "But we didn't care. We were breathing the air they were breathing. We were in eighth grade, most of us. It comes pretty close to being the highlight of my childhood." Back in Harrison, after the show, they all stopped at the Frisch's, and Ranz bought a promotional Beatles insulated tumbler.

Another person who made a pilgrimage to see the Beatles was Rose Slezak (now Rose Huber), a seventeen-year-old Middletown resident awaiting the start of her senior year at Fenwick High School. Her parents owned the city's well-known Clock Restaurant and Catering. She and her four girlfriends, as well as her brother and his two friends, crowded into the family's old Dodge station wagon for the long trip to see the Beatles. Her father, who drove, brought along a golfing buddy to kill time while the kids saw the show. When the *Cincinnati Enquirer*'s John Kiesewetter wrote a fiftieth anniversary story in 2014, Huber submitted her remembrances. The following is a previously unpublished excerpt:

> *By the time my brother and friends ordered tickets, only "standing room" passes were left (at $2.75)—just about what I thought my imposing brother and his young cohorts deserved. But he got the last laugh. His tickets were directly behind the Beatles on stage! They got to see and hear everything. We girls, standing on the folding chairs, neither heard nor saw the Beatles. All I remember is insane nonstop screaming/crying and a light show of flashbulbs going off in a blinding, continuous spectacle.*

By August 1964, the Beatles' breakneck pace of scoring American hit records had slowed, although the hits they did have were still enormous. However, they had found a replacement for top 40 domination: they were then movie stars. Their lively film *A Hard Day's Night* had been released in July and was an instant hit, garnering rave reviews for the group members' quick-witted humor. The Beatles were then winning over adults. (You can see flashes of the Beatles' humor on display when watching the preshow press conference at Cincinnati Gardens, part of that DVD assembled from the 1964 tour footage. When a reporter prefaces a question by saying, "Ringo, you've done a lot of, let's say, slapstick work in the picture," Starr tells his fellow Beatles, "Let's say 'slapstick,' 1-2-3.")

Max Elkus's late father, Robert, bought concert tickets for thirteen-year-old Max, Max's sister Nancy and a neighbor. He found excellent floor seats for them close to the stage. And, without a paid ticket, he got into the Gardens to see the Beatles himself. The fact that he owned the high-fashion Dino's Men's Clothing Store and knew promoter Dino Santangelo may have played a role in his getting into the show. He wanted to know what this young rock 'n' roll band was like. "Our seats were floor seats—we were within the first fifteen rows, and they were right there," Max Elkus said. "Once the concert started, somebody came out and said 'Beatles,' and everybody stood up. We could see them. You had to stand up, but they were right there. But it was loud." Today, Elkus wonders what his father—an open-minded jazz fan whose store hosted a WNOP remote broadcast— thought of the show. "Obviously, it was a different sound than what his generation was used to, but Dad liked all types of music. He never pointed it out to us that, like, that was amazing, but I'm betting if I could ask him today, he'd say he liked it."

The Beatles' concert was such a big deal that various representatives of Cincinnati's establishment culture weighed in. The influential newspaper the *Enquirer* ran a front-page story with a headline so hilariously square that it has acquired its own following: "Teen-agers Revel in Madness: Young Fans Drop Veneer of Civilization for Beatles." In 2016, *Enquirer* reporter Jordan Kellogg devoted a full article to remembering that story, which didn't have a byline. "It starts with the headline and only gets better," Kellogg wrote. (The *Dayton Daily News*, on the other hand, came up with something very clever: "Cincy Intact Despite the Beatles.")

Hamilton County Juvenile Court judge Benjamin Schwartz got all upset about the show, filming a bizarre statement in front of the Ohio state seal. (I first wrote about this for the *Enquirer* in 2014.) In his statement, he said he was angry that parents let their underage daughters attend an event where they could engage in loud emotional release, which he saw as having sexual overtones. "These girls went into a coma," he objected. "They ranted, they fainted. Their eyes were glassy. Some pulled their hair out. Some tore their dresses. They threw notes of a very undesirable nature on stage. Some girls, after the performance, kissed the stage. Some kissed the very seats in which the Beatles had sat." He concluded with a chilling analogy: "I believe a dictionary definition of a Beatle is a bug. Of course, bug also means being crazy. I don't think the Beatles are bugs…[but] I think the parents are bugs to let their children go to a production of this kind." And he beseeched his intended audience—presumably parents of teenagers—to not let anything like this happen again. "I think we can all agree the show was not good. Why must we have it?"

His short address is available on YouTube, as well as on the DVD *On Tour with the Beatles from LA to Philadelphia*. The latter also contains an interview with Howard Lyman, a University of Cincinnati associate professor of psychology and president-elect of the Ohio Psychological Association, who good-naturedly explained that the Beatles posed no threat to society. (Much of the DVD's Cincinnati footage, including the Lyman interview, was shot by a company called Barbre Productions, which was following the Beatles on tour until they were asked to leave, according to John C. Winn's book *Way Beyond Compare: The Beatles Recording Legacy Volume One, 1957–1965*.) Lyman offered some wisdom that sounds especially apt today:

> *I think that the young people who fall in love with the Beatles and scream at the Beatles are going to grow up to be every bit as normal as you and I. I've heard some people who think it is positively shocking the way a whole auditorium of youngsters goes into mild hysterics, or perhaps wild hysterics, at the first sound of the music and then continue all the way through the musical number. I'd like to remind [them] you can find the same facial expressions if you go to any football or basketball game. You'll find people carried away in just such rapture as you'd see in a group of teenagers at a Beatles show.*

Incidentally, it's tough to find anyone who went to the 1964 concert who has a clear, detailed remembrance of the opening acts: Bill Black's Combo, the Exciters, the Righteous Brothers and Jackie DeShannon. But two of the acts, though American, had some interesting connections with the then-raging British Invasion. DeShannon had first recorded both "Needles and Pins" and her own composition "When You Walk in the Room" in 1963;

the British band the Searchers turned them both into major U.S. hits in 1964. The Exciters, a Black "girl group" (though with one male singer) who had a hit with 1962's "Tell Him," flopped with their 1963 recording of "Do Wah Diddy Diddy." However, the British band Manfred Mann revived it and scored a no. 1 U.S. hit right around the time of the Beatles' Cincinnati Gardens concert. Meanwhile, the Righteous Brothers—Bill Medley and Bobby Hatfield—had already had a moderate hit, the danceable "Little Latin Lupe Lu," when they opened for the Beatles. But they were still months away from releasing their classic "You've Lost that Lovin' Feelin'," probably as memorable a song today as any single Beatles hit. "I love the Righteous Brothers," Elkus said, learning from this interviewer they were on the bill. "I wish I could have remembered them."

The Beatles' 1966 return to Cincinnati was a more complicated affair than their 1964 visit. Santangelo, working with the WSAI deejay Steve Kirk, booked the band to play Crosley Field on a prime Saturday night, August 20. They would be playing with opening acts the Remains, the Cyrkle, Bobby Hebb and the Ronettes (without their usual lead singer Ronnie Spector). But a rainstorm forced a cancellation after a two-hour

The happy crowd of (mostly) girls at the 1966 Beatles concert at Crosley Field. *Photograph by Fred Straub; courtesy of the* Cincinnati Enquirer.

Above: Sitting and screaming for the Fab Four at Crosley Field. *Photograph by Fred Straub; courtesy of the* Cincinnati Enquirer.

Left: Paul and John share a microphone. *Photograph by Fred Straub; courtesy of the* Cincinnati Enquirer.

Left: George Harrison at Crosley Field. *Photograph by Fred Straub; courtesy of the* Cincinnati Enquirer.

Below: Ringo Starr was a crowd favorite. *Photograph by Fred Straub; courtesy of the* Cincinnati Enquirer.

Above: Cincinnati police face the crowd at the Beatles concert. *Photograph by Fred Straub; courtesy of the* Cincinnati Enquirer.

Left: A girl with binoculars screams for the Beatles. *Photograph by Fred Straub; courtesy of the* Cincinnati Enquirer.

The well-protected stage at second base for the Beatles. *Photograph by Fred Straub; courtesy of the Cincinnati Enquirer.*

delay. Fortunately, the Beatles agreed to stay over at the Vernon Manor Hotel and play at noon on August 21 before flying out for a show in St. Louis that evening.

The Beatles were making better music than ever—their September 1966 album *Revolver* is easily one of their best, and their single releases of that year, such as "Nowhere Man," Paperback Writer," "Rain," "Yellow Submarine" and "Eleanor Rigby" showed an astonishing growth in their musical sophistication from 1964. But with that creative breakthrough came dissatisfaction: the crude sound systems of large venues and the screaming concert attendees did not showcase the music as they wished. The year 1966 marked the end of the Beatles' touring; afterward, they threw their energy into the studio, as stressed in Ron Howard's 2016 documentary, *The Beatles: Eight Days a Week—The Touring Years.* In August 1966, the Beatles performed in fourteen North American cities. The last tour date, an August 29 show at San Francisco's Candlestick Park, was basically the group's last live show ever, save for an unannounced set performed on the rooftop of London's Apple Corps building in 1969 for use in the film *Let It Be* and also planned (as this book goes to print) for Peter Jackson's 2021 television special *Get Back.*

Making the tour harder for the group was John Lennon's remark in March to Britain's *Evening Standard* newspaper that the Beatles were more popular than Jesus. This caused an uproar in the United States when the magazine *Datebook* published it at the end of July. In fact, the online Beatles Bible humorously notes that on August 13, a Texas radio station, KLUE, organized a bonfire of Beatles records and, on August 14, was struck by lightning. According to *Cincinnati Post* entertainment writer Dale Stevens, Cincinnati's concert promoters renegotiated their concert guarantee from $75,000 to $50,000 because Lennon's remark would hurt sales. (Other promoters did the same, Stevens said.) Crosley Field had a capacity of about thirty thousand; the show sold about fifteen thousand tickets.

Santangelo told me in 1986, during an interview not long before his death, "I guess I'm one of the few promoters who lost money with the Beatles." The problem, he said, was that rainstorm and the fact that the stage on the field did not have a canopy. "I and [Beatles manager] Brian Epstein had a meeting. Brian said they were afraid the instruments might not be grounded," Santangelo explained. While the Beatles didn't charge extra, Santangelo said, the additional stadium rental and labor costs caused him to lose money.

Thankfully, Sunday (August 21) was sunny, and about ten thousand fans made it back to Crosley Field. After the opening acts played—including Hebb, who appropriately sang his big hit "Sunny"—the Beatles ran out from a dugout to their stage at second base and performed Chuck Berry's "Rock and Roll Music" and their own "She's a Woman," "If I Needed Someone," "Day Tripper," "Baby's in Black," "I Feel Fine," "Yesterday," "I Wanna Be Your Man," "Nowhere Man" and "Paperback Writer" before finishing with Little Richard's "Long Tall Sally."

The *Post*'s Stevens, though an entertainment writer, revealed that he had quite the eye for sartorial observation with his concert report. Noting the band members wore plum-striped gray suits with trouser legs tapered into a slight bellbottom-like flare, he went on to describe the yellow tint in John Lennon's sunglasses and the round "granny glasses" worn by George Harrison. But he wasn't finished appraising their apparel, further noting Paul McCartney's boots, Harrison's moccasins, Lennon's "smart pair" of red suede shoes and Ringo Starr's "ordinary" pair of dress shoes. Finally, he said, "John Lennon crooks his neck like a Balinese dancer as he performs."

Among the crowd was sixteen-year-old Beverly Moeller (now Beverly Olthaus), a McAuley High School student from Mount Healthy. Olthaus at that time wrote several quite touching journal entries about the Crosley Field show and what it meant to her. Her journal provides a good description of what fans endured that wet Saturday night and also how the Sunday show provided compensation for their troubles. Olthaus had already attended the 1964 concert at Cincinnati Gardens; her aunt had bought her a ticket as a gift. (She still has the canceled check her aunt wrote to "Beatles.") Olthaus wasn't planning to see the 1966 show, but fate intervened at (literally) the last minute. The following are excerpts from the journal:

I am not going to see the Beatles on Aug. 20. Mom says it's a waste of money. You can't imagine how disappointed I was. It would put a welcome tap on the summer vacation. Although I can't see them, WSAI will give full coverage, and maybe I can feel some relief. This is said to be their last tour of the U.S. Cincy is lucky to have them. The Cyrkle is also coming with them.

Then the surprise good news arrived, courtesy of a girlfriend's father:

I don't believe it. It can't be true. At precisely 8 [p.m.] Saturday, Aug. 20, 1966, I was listening to WSAI reporting on the big Beatles show scheduled for that night. Every time I thought they would be here at Crosley Field and I wouldn't see them, well it kind of made me sick. Just as I was feeling sorry for myself, the telephone rang. "Hello, Beverly, this is Mr. Scheurmann. Would you like to see The Beatles?" I could not believe my ears. I thought it was a joke. But as I found out later, he was serious. Frantically, I hollered down to mom and asked if I could go. She said, "I don't care, go on." Three minutes to get dressed and ready to go. I don't know how I did it, but I did.

It turned out Beverly's friend Debbie, Mr. Scheurmann's daughter, and Debbie's cousin Nancy were at Crosley Field, waiting for the show, when Nancy got sick and had to go home. Debbie's father was going to have to drive down from Mount Healthy to get her, and Debbie thought Beverly would like the suddenly available complimentary ticket.

Well, we got down to Crosley Field through Portal 7 and got into our seats, which were opposite third base and in the fourth row back from the fence. They were lower box seats. And that's precisely when the rain started, and it came and came and came. For two hours, we sat in the pouring rain, drenched through and through. We moved under the roof when we met (two friends) at the telephone booth. They said they were sitting by two vacant seats in front of them when the people left. So, we sat there, protected for a time. Three minutes later, a WSAI DJ announced there was condensation in the instruments from the rain and it was possible the Beatles might be electrocuted. Therefore, the concert was canceled, to be held at noon, the next day, Sunday.

Nancy remained sick on Sunday, so Beverly got a second chance to use her ticket.

We played it safe and donned casual clothes and a pair of binoculars and a raincoat just in case. There were a lot of false alarms that the Beatles were up in the deserted bleachers, watching the crowds. The Remains were featured first. Very good guitar players, lousy looks. The man who sang "Sunny" [Hebb] was there and also the Cyrkle. The Cyrkle is one of the very best groups around today. They sang "Red Rubber Ball" and "Turn Down Day." The Ronettes were also there.

Then they came. Being not too far away from their exit place, I actually saw them very close up. Need I mention the screams and the flashbulbs? Paul stood on our side in full view. He wore a gray-and-white striped suit. He looked happy and handsome. The first song by John was "Rock & Roll Music." After each song was over, each Beatle spoke. The crowd quieted miraculously.

Need I say that they were GREAT? I know Paul looked right at me when I was waving and waved right back. Every time he turned to our section, we waved and so did he. George waved once. Ringo was hidden by the amplifiers mostly, but he did look cute. Screaming but not deafening, we heard them very well. Most of the policemen—50 just on our side— had cotton in their ears. We saw a hysterical girl screaming "Oh, Paul!" When "Long Tall Sally" was finished, they said goodbye, got in a car through a door on the right side of the scoreboard, waved white towels and disappeared. Before the Beatles left, at the end of the row, a girl three rows in front of us jumped the fence and headed for the Beatles' car. She dodged three policemen but was finally caught. I cried when they left, only a few minutes, but when you think you'll never see them again...

And she did not—there was never another chance, although Olthaus did see McCartney at U.S. Bank Arena in 2016. "I still feel like I was so blessed to see the Beatles not once but twice," Olthaus told me. "And then Paul, too." By the way, later in life, Olthaus's mother enjoyed hearing Beatles records.

10

HYDE PARK-MOUNT LOOKOUT TEEN CENTER

*T*he career of Cincinnati's most famous concert promoter, Jim Tarbell, began in 1967, when he was a cook and lookout for a fishing crew that caught swordfish in the Atlantic Ocean off the village of Galilee, Rhode Island. It was the fifth year that Tarbell had been living in New England—he had come from Cincinnati at the age of twenty-two to pursue a medical career and somehow had transitioned to become a seagoing adventurer. "The captain was one of the few guys left that hand-harpooned for swordfish. He had a sixty-five-foot trawler," Tarbell recalled.

When not cooking, Tarbell would climb to the boat's crow's nest and scout for swordfish, which can weigh up to one thousand pounds, according to *Encyclopedia Britannica*. Then the crew's "striker" would walk with the harpoon, a long oak pole with an embedded steel rod at one end and a dart and rope attached to that. When the dart found its target, the battle would begin. "It was literally hand-to-hand combat," Tarbell said. "It was too exciting."

Single, with money to spend and a red beard that made him look like a romantic "old salt," Tarbell would seem to be in an enviable position to enjoy a good off-hours social life. But there really weren't off-hours—at least not the kind you could make plans for. The crew was on call.

Then one day, just before reporting for duty, an unexpected letter from Cincinnati arrived at the small waterfront cottage Tarbell rented. He took

A poster for the Grateful Dead at Hyde Park Teen Center. *Courtesy of Bill Westheimer.*

it with him on the fishing trip and read it when they were sixty miles out at sea. It was from Frank Cone, a member of the adult advisory board of Church of the Redeemer Youth Group. Tarbell recited the letter to me, as if it's still memorized, all these decades later: "We're building a new teen center in Hyde Park, and we bought a building that was vacant. Somebody suggested you might be interested in being the director." (The group also had a separate youth board.)

So began Tarbell's stewardship of the Hyde Park–Mount Lookout Teen Center, also known as Hyde Park Teen Center. In its short existence, the center was responsible for bringing the wildly countercultural and musically experimental psychedelic drug–exploring San Francisco band Grateful Dead to Cincinnati on the group's first U.S. tour. It was 1968; the Dead had just released their second album, *Anthem of the Sun*, an experimental work that was far removed from the world of top 40 hits, but it was perfect for the then-new progressive rock programming on FM radio stations like Cincinnati's WEBN.

Talk about venturing into the belly of the beast—not only was the Haight-Ashbury-based Dead in one of the Midwest's more conservative cities, but they were also in Cincinnati's most prestigiously bourgeois neighborhood, appearing at a club financed by some of the city's wealthiest and most important citizens to keep their kids out of trouble amid the tumultuous youth revolution of the times. "They were blue blood Cincinnatians," Tarbell said. "The board of adult directors included the vice-president of Kroger, the president of Emery Industries, an executive vice-president of Procter & Gamble." (I first interviewed Tarbell about the club for a 2016 *Cincinnati Enquirer* history story and then had subsequent conversations.)

As Tarbell is quoted in *Lost Live Dead*, a blog devoted to illuminating the Grateful Dead's shows that are either "unknown or poorly documented," "You can still see people wandering up and down Erie Avenue with smiles on their faces, wondering what happened. It was the Grateful Dead and all they embody, which was a little extreme for Cincinnati at the time. They were two hours late, and they played for three hours. They were running around, chasing teenage girls. People were literally hanging from the rafters."

If you're wondering why Hyde Park and Mount Lookout blue bloods turned to a Rhode Island fisherman to run their new teen center, Tarbell speculated his mother might have suggested him when she heard they were looking. He had grown up in Hyde Park, and in 1957, when he was fifteen, he had proposed a Hyde Park teen center to the Cincinnati Recreation Commission. "Myself and other ragamuffins were hanging out in the [neighborhood] square," he explained. "My father was dead and my mother working, and there was nothing to go home to. And the merchants were not happy. So I said, 'Why don't you do a way station for us, and we'll get out of your hair?'" He even knew a place, an old church at 2753 Erie Avenue that the city had bought to use as a parking lot but then changed its mind. As fate would have it, it was that building that the new youth group's adult board had bought. The Episcopalian Church of the Redeemer, also on Erie Avenue, had already acquired a citywide reputation for hosting youth dances with local bands that covered garage rock and British Invasion hits and was comfortable with the notion that live rock music would play a role at the new center.

The *Cincinnati Enquirer*'s Saturday teen-ager section eagerly followed the developments. In its June 22, 1968 issue, the *Enquirer* recounted the long road to the club's upcoming opening on Friday, June 28. Over the course of two years, at first with interim director Rink Smith, the organizers had created a capital fund to raise $135,000 (remodeling costs totaled $75,000); this included selling Christmas trees and raising $200 per holiday by making deliveries for area florists. The adult advisory board, meanwhile, solicited donations. The article stated that "a main purpose of the teen center is to hold dances with live entertainment" but that the place also wanted to recognize "youth's intense concern with the present and the future. It is an organization that senses existing social problems and will take an active part in trying to solve them through community commitment. It will be proving ground for [a] teenager's responsibility, initiative and intellectual and artistic abilities." As Tarbell explained to me, "The whole idea was to give these kids authority—to let them be involved. And they were wonderful. They deserve credit."

The teen center also set up membership requirements, as it was trying to be relatively inclusive while also first serving the youths who first supported it. You could buy a membership if you either:

- Lived in postal zones 08 or 26 and were in grades nine through twelve.
- Were in grades nine through twelve at the Withrow, Marian or Summit Country Day Schools.
- Were not in school but lived in those zones and were no older than eighteen.

A member could sponsor two guests per year, and there were also group memberships available to church groups, fraternities and sororities.

The old church proved a good fit for a music venue—the sanctuary was spacious, and the site of the raised altar lent itself to being a stage. In anticipation of loud local rock bands, interior designer Patrick Korb suggested placing soft, bumpy egg cartons on the walls. They were painted black and white for some pizazz. There was also what Tarbell describes as an interior dome.

While the teen center was primarily meant to host local bands, its young supporters wanted to make a big initial splash. So, opening night started with a national act. Vanilla Fudge from Long Island had had tremendous success in the fall of 1967 and into 1968 with sludgy, hypnotically slow versions of songs like the Supremes's "You Keep Me Hanging On" and the Beatles's "Eleanor Rigby." It was one of the first acts to be discovered by FM progressive rock stations, especially the then-new WEBN, and subsequently became so big that the top 40 embraced them. "I thought it was a good place to start, at the low end of a national band price, $2,000," Tarbell said.

Vanilla Fudge (with local act Ivan & the Sabers as their opener) was maybe too good of a place to start—the band sold out the place, which could hold about two hundred people, and left more outside who were trying to get in. In the July 6, 1968 edition of the *Enquirer*'s teen-ager section, two nonmembers who couldn't get inside wrote a letter charging discrimination. Teen center president Roger Berliner answered the next week, saying the building was packed to capacity solely with members and guests and that "we are not big enough to serve the entire Cincinnati area."

Afterward, the center did feature local bands. And Tarbell, during the summer, took a trip to San Francisco to see what was happening musically there. He went to the Avalon Ballroom, where he saw Jefferson Airplane. "Then I heard about the Grateful Dead," he said. "I didn't hear them in person, but what I heard on a recording sounded interesting. I thought they'd be an interesting way to get people to the teen center." He contacted the band's manager, who said the Dead were doing their first road trip through America and would be coming Tarbell's way in November. The band was booked for Thanksgiving weekend.

One of the hardest things about documenting the Dead's teen center concert has been figuring out which nights the group played and how many shows they performed, as there are conflicting records. But based on the *Enquirer*'s teen-ager section's coverage, my own interviews and the work done by the blog *Lost Live Dead*, it appears they did three shows over two nights, on Friday and Saturday, November 29 and 30. They may have been planning a fourth but had arrived in town too late to do it.

The November 29 show was only for teen center members and their guests, while the two November 30 shows were for the general public. A teen center member explained this policy change in a letter to the teen-ager section's November 9 edition, urging people to buy November 30 tickets in advance to avoid being turned away at the door. The writer, D.J. Weber, also spurred interest by claiming "this will probably be the last Midwest concert for the group, since they are breaking up in December." (This did not happen.) Weber also said there would be two shows on November 29, just for members and guests.

As it sometimes happens with these things, with time, accounts differ. (There are sound recordings of the band's November 22, 1968 show at Veterans Memorial Auditorium in Columbus and their December 7, 1968 performance at Bellarmine College in Louisville to give an approximate indication of their repertoire.)

The Dead lineup included guitarist extraordinaire/vocalist Jerry Garcia, rhythm guitarist and vocalist Bob Weir, bassist Phil Lesh, drummers Bill Kreutzmann and Mickey Hart, keyboardist Tom Constanten and keyboardist/percussionist/vocalist Ron "Pigpen" McKernan. And along as the sound mixer was Kentucky native Augustus Owsley Stanley III, who also had a now-fabled ability to manufacture LSD.

Constanten, the Dead's new fulltime keyboardist at the time, told me for a 2016 *Enquirer* story that the Cincinnati gig was notable because he and the Dead's first keyboardist, Pigpen, both played there. "It was possible it was the only time Pigpen and I played keyboards at the same time," he said. "It was a multi-tiered stage—drums were highest, next were keyboards and lowest and closest to the audience was the guitars." Constanten remembered that his presence "liberated" Pigpen to step forward as a front man, playing congas and singing energetic R&B numbers like "Turn on Your Love Light." "The Dead were two bands—when Jerry fronted or when Pigpen fronted," he said. (Pigpen stayed with the Dead in his new role until 1972; he died in 1973.)

Some insight into the excitement that accompanied the band's appearance—and also the fact that things didn't exactly occur with pinpoint punctuality—can be gleaned from an article in the December 7 teenager section of the *Enquirer*, in which writer Bob Buten wrote about his frustrated attempts to interview band members. It was headlined "Bob has a Lost Weekend—Or the Interview that Never Was." In the article, Buten recounts how he arrived at 7:30 p.m. on November 29 for the 8:00 p.m. concert and found only himself and teen-ager reporter Jim Knippenberg present. When the doors finally opened and he got inside, he was booted out by teen center members as a freeloader. Tarbell subsequently arranged for Buten to interview the band at 1:30 p.m. the next day. Buten was there, but the band didn't show up until 5:00 p.m. No interview occurred, but he did get to attend the scheduled 10:00 p.m. show, which started at 11:00 p.m. and consisted of "three tremendous songs."

Knippenberg separately wrote a review that—while it never mentioned any band members or songs by name—beautifully and vividly captured its essence, as well as the changes going through rock, and all of America, at the time. The following is an excerpt:

> *Because you can feel the vibration of every drumbeat, because your eardrum feels the reverberation of every guitar scream, because every progression on the keyboard rattles your brain, because every swirl of light covers your and the performer's face and captures your eyes, because everyone is so close together and so near the stage, because everyone is lorded over by some huge communal over-soul, you don't watch a Grateful Dead concert, you participate.*
>
> *It is also these very same things which work together to make a great concert, and which also help to make rock music one of the most exciting, alive and ever-explosive fields on the horizon today.*

The "swirl of light" that Knippenberg refers to was a very sophisticated light show produced by several Cincinnati teenagers known collectively as FlavorScope (sometimes spelled as Flavor Scope or Flavorscope). They had debuted at the Vanilla Fudge concert, but the Dead were their baptism by fire and the first time they used the FlavorScope name. They set up a projection booth overlooking the concert space and the band, and they set about manipulating the equipment. One of the original FlavorScope members, University of Kansas religion professor Daniel Stevenson, wrote a detailed description on *Lost Live Dead*:

> *The Dead did show up late on Friday night, with Owsley on sound....On Friday night, they started with a rather sloppy version of "Good Morning Little School Girl," but in short order got into the groove and blew the roof off the place, at least to my recollection.*
>
> *This was our first gig as FlavorScope Lightshow. We were pretty green at the time. We literally set up in the rafters of the church and projected through a window carved into the domed ceiling. I remember, at one point, sticking my head out—figuratively and literally—and hearing music that changed my life. ("That's It for the Other One" and "New Potato Caboose," etc.)*
>
> *On Saturday, we gathered mid-morning at the center to tweak equipment. The Dead showed up and proceeded to practice and jam until late afternoon. I remember Mickey Hart and Bill Kreutzmann working out dual drum*

solos, as other members came and went. Bob Weir, at one point, did a rendition of "Silver Threads and Golden Needles." There are other details which I will not recount. Pigpen was a damned nice guy, as were all.

Another member of the FlavorScope group, Johnathon Crawford, recalled some highlights in an interview with me. (He had become a marketing director for a Milwaukee communications firm):

In the light show business, we used a lot of liquids to make psychedelic imagery. We would float colored mineral oil on top of water to create beautiful psychedelic patterns. We used to buy Squib Mineral Oil by the case. Tarbell came to me and said, "Jerry Garcia needs some oil." I said, "I've got some mineral oil," and Garcia shouted from the bottom of this ladder, because we were up in the attic area and there was just a trap door and ladder, that that would work great. So, I got him a fresh bottle of mineral oil, and I remember him coming up the ladder and handing him the oil. And he was missing a finger. First time I had ever realized he was a guitar player missing a finger. He wanted mineral oil for his hands to play so he could play faster, and it would improve his musicianship. [Garcia had lost the top half of the middle finger of his right hand in a childhood wood-chopping accident.]

The other two FlavorScope founders were Bill Westheimer, now a highly regarded photographer, and the late Jamie Osher. They also had assistants.

The Grateful Dead concerts were the teen center's highlights. Afterward, it continued to present local acts and petered out around the spring of 1969. Tarbell has said it was just too small for the growing demand of live rock. He had left the center after Christmas in 1968 and started to look for his own rock club. "I think the ability to appeal to a larger audience was part of it," he said. "I thought a new scene was emerging, and it wasn't going to stop anytime soon. It was way too exciting." He found that new place in 1969—Ludlow Garage, which is as important a lost Cincinnati milestone to boomers as the Big Red Machine championship baseball teams of the mid-1970s. But that's for a later chapter.

Meanwhile, before we leave the courageously innovative Hyde Park Teen Center, the following are the last words from the teenager section's Buten, who spent that lost weekend trying to interview the Dead. It appears he did at least get to talk to Stanley, the sound mixer, after the show on November 30 finished and the Dead's first Cincinnati visit was almost history:

After the concert was over, the whole group went downstairs and ate fruit. It looked so good, I had a few pieces myself. Would you believe I finally got to one of the Grateful Dead group, and I asked him what he was supposed to do while his buddies played their instruments. (You see, he just stood on stage and jumped around with a mic that wasn't plugged in, so I was curious.) I didn't get much of an answer, but he seemed like a pretty good guy. Soon, they all disappeared, one by one, until there wasn't anyone left in the room. So, I left, too.

11

BLACK DOME

*L*udlow Garage, the subject of the next chapter, was Cincinnati's most transformative concert venue during the 1960s. It was a phantasmagoria of a hippie rock club, whose very name still conjures visions of a utopian time and place. The Garage's importance to Cincinnati during its short period of operation—September 1969 to January 1971—can't be overstated. Someday, it should have its own permanent exhibit at the Cincinnati History Museum. But Ludlow Garage was not the first high-profile Cincinnati club that reflected the social, cultural and musical changes of the era. That honor belongs to the Black Dome, which was near the University of Cincinnati (UC) at 2506 Vine Street and operated throughout much of 1969.

Although the Black Dome was near UC, advertising its location as "Calhoun and Vine," it was not one of the beery clubs with live local music that were so popular with college students. It drew a different, citywide audience—"heads," to use a popular term of the era—with its all-ages format, lack of alcohol and the fact that it was open all night, several days a week. The Dome booked the new wave of national and international musicians who appealed to the Woodstock generation (a term not yet coined when the Dome opened) and listeners of the creative, groundbreaking FM rock being that was being played on WEBN. "It was the hip place to hang out," said Richard Von Nida, whose local band Quick Quick played there. "It was known all over the city that it was the place to go."

A Black Dome poster for Dr. John, the Night Tripper. *Courtesy of Richard Von Nida.*

Among the national acts that performed at the Dome were Dr. John, the Night Tripper, an artist who dressed in a resplendent New Orleans voodoo shaman costume and sang spooky songs like "I Walk on Gilded Splinters"; album-oriented rock heroes Procol Harum; Cleveland newcomers the James Gang, with hotshot guitarist Joe Walsh; Taj Mahal, the young Black man who was reinventing the blues for his own generation; and the older John Mayall, who had done the same for the blues in England. And there were rockers who are less known today than those mentioned above but who are enthusiastically remembered by those who saw them at Black Dome—Earth Opera, the Insect Trust and Rhinoceros, for example.

"We could walk or wander down there at two or three in the morning and [Cincinnati band] Sacred Mushroom might be playing [the] blues, or Ivan and the Sabers might come on," recalled longtime radio personality Brian O'Donnell, who had graduated from Purcell High School in 1969 and was working while living in Golf Manor. "It was remarkable to me. That's how it was many Friday and Saturday nights at the Dome."

O'Donnell fondly described one of his favorite shows at the Dome by the Boston band Earth Opera, who combined rock and folk instrumentation with driving horns on an epic protest song against the Vietnam War called "American Eagle Tragedy." In the band were singer/guitarist/saxophonist Peter Rowan and mandolinist/multi-instrumentalist David Grisman, two of the top bluegrass players today. "That was a monster concert," O'Donnell said. "I got a chance to interview Peter many years later, when I was working at WNKU (a defunct folk/Americana station at Northern Kentucky University), and when I brought up Earth Opera at Black Dome, he loved it. He was very proud of that work he did then."

The Dome's history is less well documented than Ludlow Garage's, since it was ahead of the curve. But the *Cincinnati Enquirer*'s excellent weekly teenager section, the *Independent Eye* and the *UC News-Record* did try to keep up. And the venue advertised its bigger-name shows.

The Black Dome owed its existence to a quirk in the social habits of UC students. The neighborhood's student-oriented bars were mostly within an area bounded to the south by West McMillan Street, the west by Clifton Avenue, the north by Calhoun Street and the east by Vine Street. The students were reluctant to travel on foot outside of that zone for nightlife, though there were exceptions. They were especially reluctant to cross busy, twisty Vine Street, the city's east–west divider, to go east to where Calhoun Street becomes William Howard Taft Road and where McMillan Street becomes East McMillan Street. That area also marked the start of Corryville, one of Cincinnati's many other neighborhoods. "For some reason, Vine [Street] was kind of a dividing line, and college kids didn't go across it," said Eugene Barnett, one of Black Dome's two principal business operators and now a Florida resident. (The other owner, John Horvath, could not be located for this story.)

But there was an alluring, unused building on Vine Street between East McMillan and Taft Streets that seemed spacious; it was a one-story-tall hall on a fifty-by-ninety-foot lot. Wedged between an apartment building to the south and a bank to the north, it was easy to miss. Barnett said he tracked down the vacant building's owners, William K. Sakkas and Sam Sakellariou, who owned the campus bar/music venue the Pickle Barrel. Barnett thought they had briefly tried to duplicate the Pickle Barrel format at the new location but couldn't draw customers. "So, I said, 'Let me lease it from you and see what I can do,'" Barnett recalled. He brought in Horvath, a friend he knew from Xavier University.

Indeed, Sakkas and Sakellariou had bought the building and tried to make a go of it as the Red Onion, which had a format similar to Pickle Barrel's. But neither the location nor the time was right, said Stan Hertzman, whose A. Jaye Entertainment booked bands and whose Umbrella Artist Management handled acts. A. Jaye had the entertainment concession at Pickle Barrel. In late June 1968, Hertzman left town for four months to do army basic training. He returned in late October to find that everything around UC had changed. And he learned that the Red Onion, which did not reflect those changes, had opened and closed while he was away. "What had gone down was the Summer of Love had come to Cincinnati a year late," Hertzman said. "It was like Haight-Ashbury. And it [the Red Onion] was not a progressive rock club. It was a bar that used bar bands."

The building at 2506 Vine Street that became Black Dome had housed the United Italian Societies Hall through 1966, according to *Williams' Cincinnati Directory*. It seems the Italian organization moved into the building from elsewhere in 1962. After 1966, the site was occasionally used by others. For instance, on March 29 and 30 and April 2, 1967, the Art Association of Cincinnati presented experimental films at 2506 Vine Street. On June 10, 1968, the Cincinnati Aquarium Society met there, offering a roundtable discussion on guppies and a "fish of the month" competition.

Barnett was young, just twenty-two, when the Dome opened for business. But he already had experience booking bands, as well as being in one, the Village Idiots. Using "Tin Man" as a production moniker, Barnett and several musician friends started offering teen dances in 1967 at Lakeridge

Hall, an event space at Banning and Pippin Roads in Groesbeck. Barnett's band was a regular presence at Friday night shows, and he was soon sponsoring live music on Sunday afternoons and Thursday nights as well. Such well-regarded local bands as the Lemon Pipers, Surdy Greebus, Ivan and the Sabers, Cykiks, Missing Link, Rastels, Salvation and the/his Army, the Checkmates and the Denems appeared, along with the Village Idiots. Barnett said:

> *It was a huge success from day one. I remember we had 1,600 kids. Three weeks prior to opening, we put up fliers and posters saying "Tin Man is coming," but we didn't say what it was. About a week before the event, we announced it as a big dance at Lakeridge Hall. I did strings of color lights across the supporting metal trusses on a motorized rotary switch, so we had lights going different colors and stuff, and we had a nice stage. I was the emcee.*

With his flair for concert promotion, Barnett soon tried to book a top 40 act as a headliner. He picked a good one. While Tommy James & the Shondells scored a no. 1 hit in the summer of 1966 with "Hanky Panky," they failed at a big follow-up. But Barnett showcased the group just as their massively successful "I Think We're Alone Now" was peaking. He had one of the hottest rock acts of the moment, and his own band got to open.

In 1968, his Tin Man moved to Kolping Grove at Winton and Compton Roads in Springfield Township—there was a financial dispute with Lakeridge Hall, Barnett told me. On Sunday afternoons, he brought in some additional national rock bands whose top 40 hits were showing a heavier, psychedelicized edge. (Rock historians now refer to such songs as "psych pop.") The Outsiders ("Time Won't Let Me") played in February, a double bill featuring Strawberry Alarm Clock ("Incense and Peppermints") and Canned Heat ("On the Road Again") was booked on March 3 and the wonderfully named Electric Prunes ("I Had Too Much to Dream Last Night") headlined a March 17 show.

But by March, Barnett was also planning something much larger. Working with Horvath and the Xavier University Student Council, he brought the red-hot Jimi Hendrix Experience to the university's Schmidt Fieldhouse on March 28, with trippy British act Soft Machine opening. Tickets ranged from $3.50 to $5.50, substantially more than the $2.00 for Electric Prunes, but it was a bargain, in retrospect, for the undisputed guitar god Hendrix. This was Hendrix's first Cincinnati show as a headliner. Barnett credits his successful Tommy James booking and subsequent top 40 hitmaker shows for the opportunity to be the promoter. "I think that's how I had the connections to buy Jimi Hendrix, because at my young age, I was booking major acts."

Originally, the Jimi Hendrix Experience was supposed to come to Cincinnati on July 28, 1967, as an opening act for top 40 kings the Monkees, in what has been called "one of the strangest pairings in rock 'n' roll history." But Hendrix left that tour after a July 16 date at Forest Hills Stadium in Queens, New York City.

After his Hendrix success, Barnett quit college to pursue business opportunities. He and Horvath were ready for something bigger—something, like Hendrix, more attuned to what was being played on WEBN, rather than the increasingly old-fashioned top 40 countdowns of AM radio. (Actually, top 40 station WSAI played Hendrix's singles; "Purple Haze" had gone top ten.)

Individual memories about how the Black Dome operated can be hazy, since everything happened more than fifty years ago, and few thought at the time the place would someday become culturally significant. Ron Volz, who was active in the local music scene as a roadie with Ivan and the Sabers and also lived near the building that became Black Dome, recalled via email and a follow-up interview how he helped Barnett locate and then create the Dome. "I found the vacant building and pried open the front door to check out the inside," said Volz, now living in California. "From my apartment next door, I could see the roof that was a dome. That's how I saw the building in the first place—looking out my apartment window." (Others interviewed, who might not have had the same view as Volz, do not recall a rooftop dome.) One key detail: Volz had painted the walls of his apartment black.

Volz said he got Ivan and the Sabers interested. He also explained that he lured Larry Butler, keyboardist and coleader of the band, into the project. Butler doesn't recall that, but he does remember seeing the place for the first time. "You walked in the front door, and there's an office, then a big ass room, bare walls, a twenty-foot ceiling and in back a kitchen of sorts," Butler, now living in Nashville, recalled. "No stage, no lights. Empty."

Volz got involved in the renovation. "I designed the interior look," he said. "Painted it black, like my apartment next door, and my girlfriend painted fluorescent butterflies on the walls while I installed black lights. Double Dome LSD was being sold on Calhoun Street at that time, and everybody knew about it. That's when I thought of the name. The Black Dome!"

Meanwhile, Butler and Ronald Rantz—who also worked for Ivan and the Sabers—took on other duties. "Larry Butler and me built the stage," said

Rantz, now living in Minneapolis. "My cousin was going to architecture school, so I persuaded him to design the stage so it would withstand a lot of people, a lot of equipment. He drew up a blueprint that Larry and I followed, so we started building a stage and put it in a corner. Larry did all the electrical wiring; I did carpentry, and Ron Volz worked as well."

As Rantz remembers the club's interior layout, patrons entered from Vine Street and walked down a narrow passageway to the large, open room, where the big stage was to their right. They passed a very small room, also on the right, that served as the office and dressing room. In the rear of the concert area, also on the right, was a door that allowed groups to bring in their equipment from East McMillan Street.

The interior of the Dome was a stark break from the UC bars of the day. When the Dome was open at night, it usually only used its black lights, although bands sometimes brought in auxiliary spotlights. The ultraviolet light in the otherwise-dark room allowed the painted butterflies to shine. There were also several narrow, vertical murals that contained variously sized circles against the windows.

Patrons could sit on folding chairs or on rugs. "They were old carpets that they'd get at thrift stores, and they'd line the floor with them," Rantz said. "But that became kind of an inconvenience, as people would spill stuff, and they'd get kind of nasty. Every now and then, Ron and I would have to roll them up and throw them out. Then Ron would go to thrift stores for other ones." With time, Rantz said, rugs and chairs grew scarcer. "Probably, there were more dates without rugs than with them," he recalled. "Even chairs were kind of at a premium. Most people were standing. It could get pretty crowded in there."

Ivan and the Sabers wound up playing there often, and Butler served as a kind of public representative for the operation. "I became a spokesman, not necessarily for the management but a front," he explained. "[The Dome] always had the image of being a musician's venue for making music only and not for making money." (He pointed out that the business's actual owners did indeed want to make money.)

Actually, stories in the *Enquirer's* teenager section reveal that Black Dome, using that name, first opened on November 16, 1968, in the building that had been home to the Mug Club College Bar at the corner of Dennis and Calhoun Streets. The Dome spent several weeks there.

The opening in the building at Dennis and Calhoun Streets was announced in a letter to the teen-ager section from Butler, which itself was a reply to a previous letter that complained there wasn't anything new to

The dark interior of Black Dome rock club. *Photograph by Mark Treitel; courtesy of the* Cincinnati Enquirer.

do in Cincinnati. "The whole affair starts about 9 p.m. and features not only a top vocal heavy rock group but also an all-night after-hour rock jam featuring the best area rock musicians doing their own thing," he wrote. "A quick check with local police got a favorable response from the officers who patrol the Calhoun Street area, especially since no alcoholic beverages will be sold." Butler also said, in the future, there would be national acts.

On November 16 and again on November 23, this version of the Dome presented Quick Quick. Also on November 23, the teenager section published a letter from Horvath, thanking the publication for its coverage and saying that 1,500 people had crowded the venue to date. Soon afterward, on November 30, the paper announced that Black Dome would be opening on December 6 at its permanent home on Vine Street.

The new Black Dome benefited early on from a major feature by teenager section writer Kathy Lang, which helped launch the club and still sounds perceptive today. The feature was in the January 11, 1969 *Enquirer*, headlined "Black Dome Swings with Rock Entertainment." Lang had attended one of the Dome's first events at the Vine Street location and was impressed—touched, really—by the crowd scene as Ivan and the Sabers and local band Stone Fox played. "The Black Dome's owners are something else, too," she wrote:

> *Their ability to understand and meet the needs of the area teenagers is fantastic. Instead of going for the ultra-sophisticated, over-18 campus hangout that seems to be the trend, they've reverted to the "underground" atmosphere of semi-darkness, kitchen chairs and espresso. After midnight, almost anyone can come up with the bands and "jam" all night if they want to.*
>
> *All around me, people sat on the rug-covered floor, laughing, talking or listening to the music. It seemed that the standard greeting for a friend was a big, sincere hug, regardless of race, age or sex.*

Lang reported the place had just opened on December 6, 1968, and already had over ten thousand total in attendance.

It wasn't long before Black Dome became Cincinnati's stop for national album rock acts. The Dome could hold up to nine hundred people for a show and had the ability, for big acts, to schedule two separately ticketed shows per night. Compiled from various printed sources, the following is a list of those who played at the Black Dome in 1969:

- February 20 and possibly February 21: Procol Harum (two shows on February 20)
- March 7 and 8: the Insect Trust
- March 14 and 15: James Gang
- March 16: John Mayall (two shows)
- April 3, 4 and 5: Rhinoceros (with James Gang on April 3 and 4)
- April 12: James Cotton
- April 18 and 19: Earth Opera (two shows per night)
- April 25, 26 and 27: Earth Opera (return engagement)
- May 3 and 4 (maybe also May 2): Sweetwater
- May 9 and 10: Taj Mahal
- May 16 and 17: Alice Cooper
- May 23 and 24: Mr. Stress Blues Band
- June 21: James Gang with Joe Walsh
- June 28: MC5 (shows at 10:00 p.m. and midnight)
- July 13: Amboy Dukes with Ted Nugent (shows at 8:00 and 10:00 p.m.)

- August 2 and 3: Dr. John, the Night Tripper
- August 16: The Litter

This list may not be definitive. The May 9–10 Taj Mahal shows were advertised as a return engagement; a *Dayton Daily News* story also mentions national acts Colwell-Winfield Blues Band, Silver Apples and a New York hard rock band called Street as having played the Dome.

The Dome continued to host local acts as openers or on nights without national headliners, and they often had good followings. Sixth Day Creation, which was really Ivan and the Sabers under an alias, made a local hit with the neo-psychedelic "Cherry Pie." Virtuoso guitarist Sandy Nassan would eventually record for jazz superstar Herbie Mann's Embryo label.

But it wasn't all rock music at the Black Dome. The club also tried to lure patrons with other attractions—a folk night on Sundays; free admission on Wednesdays; hot dogs, bagels and peanut butter and jelly sandwiches at the refreshment stand. And for some, there was also the allure of drugs. Butler said he used to make an announcement from the stage that "every night is narc night. No holding at the Black Dome." By email, he added, "The authorities were rabid to find a reason to close us down. Never happened, so I guess my warning worked."

There were also attempts—or at least discussions in the press—to create a local curfew for teens. Beatles-hating juvenile court judge Benjamin Schwartz warned minors to stop gathering along Calhoun Street, which had a reputation for drug use, but the Cincinnati ACLU accused him of trying to exert excessive authority.

For some of the national acts, Black Dome was a stepping-stone, a veritable stairway to heaven. When Walsh's James Gang first appeared in March 1969, the group needed to combat their lack of a following by being introduced in a newspaper advertisement as "three-piece progressive blues from Cleveland." (However, there exists online a posting from Seymour Duncan, a veteran guitarist and owner of a California company that makes guitar and bass pickups, about playing Yardbirds songs with Walsh at the Mug Club after Duncan moved to Cincinnati in 1966.)

The James Gang turned out to be one of the Black Dome's most popular acts, and they built a strong following in Cincinnati by giving free performances at Eden Park and Clifton's Mount Storm Park in 1969. Barnett recalled an experience after he left Cincinnati for Los Angeles in the autumn of 1969. "I was standing at the Whisky-a-Go-Go one night, and I hear this voice going, 'Hey, Barnett.' I turn around, and it's Joe Walsh. He said, 'Man, your club's the best club I ever played.'"

When Taj Mahal played Black Dome, he was still on the verge of a breakthrough that his 1969 album, *Giant Step/De Ole Folks at Home*, soon provided. Today, Taj Mahal is an elder of Americana music. In a 2011 interview with *Enquirer* writer Paul Clark, he recalled the boost he got from the enthusiastic crowd members (I was one) at his Black Dome shows. "Listen, the Black Dome was the first place I knew [my music] was taking off and reaching people," he said. "I was looking off the stage at the Black Dome, and the place was filled. They put more people in there than was allowed. The walls were sweating."

Stu Levy, a UC student who was also a photographer who had played in the band Surdy Grebus, accompanied Detroit's raucously loud, high-energy MC5 to their Black Dome shows and documented the trip. The band was accompanied by their mentor, the music critic and radical theorist John Sinclair, the founder of the White Panther Party. "He carried around Mao's *Little Red Book* and he [had] a big black beard," Levy said. "He was a pretty charismatic character. MC5 were a quite phenomenal group—pre-punk, radical, amazing musicians who put on a quite frenzied show. They were just something else."

Detroit's high-energy band MC5 backstage at Black Dome. *Photograph by Stu Levy.*

Levy recalls driving to Detroit to see the band with Frank Wood Jr., who introduced "underground" rock on WEBN and hosted its signature *Jelly Pudding* program. (Wood was also the son of the station owner.) Wood said he doesn't recall going with Levy but definitely remembers the trip. "The MC5 were very big on the radio station for a very short time," he said. "All I remember was it was the loudest concert I ever went to in my life. My ears rang all the way back."

Probably the most impressive booking in the club's short history was bringing British band Procol Harum to Cincinnati. The band was advertised to play two shows on February 20, 1969, but appears to have stayed over for a second night. Procol Harum had already released a hit single of monumental proportions, 1967's "A Whiter Shade of Pale." It had all the elements of a classic: colorfully evocative and mysteriously alluring lyrics written by Keith Reid, a melody that unfurled with a stately Baroque grandeur (courtesy of the way it borrowed from Bach), Matthew Fisher's mournfully prominent Hammond organ part and Gary Brooker's rough-hewn and impassioned vocals and piano work. By 1969, Procol Harum had also encouraged a bluesy, urgent rock 'n' roll edge from guitarist Robin Trower, complemented by solid drummer B.J. Wilson. They were earning comparisons to the American group the Band for their earthy, gritty side.

Procol Harum also had something special going for them in Cincinnati. WEBN's linchpin *Jelly Pudding* had adopted the group's elegiac "Repent Walpurgis" as its theme. This was a Fisher-composed instrumental with a forebodingly forceful, slightly eerie melody that could be classified as early progressive rock. Wood described the song to me as having a Halloween vibe. "It made a good way to begin and end *Jelly Pudding*," he said. "They were a good band—I liked their music; it was very interesting."

Rantz recalled picking up Procol Harum's equipment at the airport. "We used the Sabers' truck that they had just purchased at the time," he recalled. "The piano was a rental that Horvath had arranged to be delivered and set up on stage. When Procol Harum arrived that day, Gary Brooker did a soundcheck. I remember it vividly because he did the song 'A Salty Dog.'" (The evocative ballad, one of the band's best songs, was featured on their album of the same name that was released in June 1969.)

The venue sold five hundred tickets (at five dollars each) for each of the February 20 shows amid keen demand. Concert attendee Brian O'Donnell remembers finding an eager, attentive crowd. "There were some seats and some Persian rugs. I was laying on a Persian rug maybe ten feet away from

Brooker's piano, and I watched the whole show from there. It was just freaking phenomenal."

Ken Hawkins, who interviewed the band for the *Independent Eye* between the two shows, remembers spending time with them on February 21. Brooker and Trower wanted to see some of the dining and drinking hotspots of Mount Adams.

"I did the interview and the shoot on their first night at the Dome," Hawkins said via email:

> *Gary and Robin wanted to go to Mount Adams—Mahogany Hall, I think—so the next day, I picked them up in my brand-new VW, and we headed up the hill. We went to Pia Battaglia's for a fine lunch of her homemade minestrone soup, then walked around Mount Adams with an early afternoon stop at the Blind Lemon, where they'd just opened for the day. A libation or three later, we drove down the hill to Trivet's Antiques and then a head shop whose name I can't recall. We then trucked on up to Price Hill to WEBN, but I don't think that Frank had made it in.*
>
> *Back to Clifton, I dropped Gary and Robin off—where, I can't recall. They had another show planned for that night, but I couldn't attend. I had a first date with the girl I ended up marrying. Long story short, I can't confirm that they played the second night, but it was planned as of late afternoon when I left them.*

Even two years later, people were still talking about Procol Harum's Black Dome shows. In 1971, writing about an upcoming Jethro Tull/Procol Harum concert at Cincinnati Gardens, *Enquirer* writer Jim Knippenberg said this about the band: "They have been to Cincinnati—to the Black Dome a few years ago—and there are lots of us who just can't forget. What we remember most is the packed club, totally stoned on the Keith Reid lyrics and the Gary Brooker keyboard work—especially the keyboard."

After mid-August, something happened at the Black Dome. The big acts stopped; the good press faded. Barnett said there was a business disagreement between him and Horvath, but he doesn't remember the details. (This was also right around the time that Ludlow Garage was planning to open.) On October 3 and 4, Horvath opened a short-lived club called Panacea at 3225 Madison Road in Oakley, with the James Gang and Lemon Pipers as his first acts. But it only lasted a short time. "Oakley was not a popular direction to go for a rock club at that time," Volz said. Horvath was also involved with partner Ronald Filburn for a short-lived rock club in Dayton called Papaliski's.

Meanwhile, Barnett tried a novel idea he called "Rock Clubs," in which nonalcoholic music events would occur at four separate locations on the same night. It debuted on Halloween in 1969, with Balderdash and the Rapscallion Sirkle at Skateaway Roller Rink in Middletown (north); the Glass Wall and the Established Revue at the American Legion Hall in Milford (east); the Haymarket Riot and Whalefeathers at Elks Hall in Cold Spring, Kentucky (south); and the Lemon Pipers and Jesse at the western location, his old standby Lakeridge Hall. Soon after, he left for California.

The Black Dome appeared in newspapers in September 1969 as the spot where the radical Students for a Democratic Society tried to recruit high schoolers by showing movies about the Black Panther Party, angering city officials. (No one interviewed for this story remembers anything about that.)

The city planned to get rid of the building, as well as the ones surrounding it, for its Avondale urban renewal project. In December 1969, the *Post* reported that the owners of the property, Sakellariou and Sakkas, went to court to contest the city's determination that they should receive just $67,000 for the site. The owners wanted $88,000; a jury awarded them $76,000.

In January 1970, Don Bates Inc. advertised a public auction of the contents, including chairs, the stage and six "abstract muriels," (probably meaning "murals"). The general area became home for, first, a U-Totem Convenience Store and, later, a CVS. But if you're of a certain age and still have the classic rock or progressive rock tastes you had in 1969, you'll more than likely hear at some point "A Whiter Shade of Pale" playing on your car radio. The venue may be lost, but the best music of the acts it presented is still very much with us.

12

LUDLOW GARAGE

*I*t was April 1969, and Carole Winters of Fort Thomas, Kentucky, wanted to see Tim Buckley, a rising folk rock singer-songwriter, in Dayton, Ohio. But she was eighteen and didn't want to drive by herself. No problem—in those days, such was the spirit of idealism within the emerging youthful counterculture that she could just request a ride via WEBN, the FM rock station that saw itself and the music it played as agents for progressive change. She did just that and got a ride offer from Jim Tarbell, who, at the age of twenty-six, had already made a name for himself by bringing San Francisco's premier psychedelic band, the Grateful Dead, to the Hyde Park Teen Center in 1968 while he had been its director. He had quit the job earlier.

A friendship developed, and Tarbell later told her about his latest plan: a rock club that could serve as a gathering place, a community center, for its youthful audience, just like the Avalon or the Fillmore Ballrooms in San Francisco. And he even knew of a potential site: an old auto repair garage at what was then 346 Ludlow Avenue in Clifton. Impressed, Winters volunteered to become part of the crew of "kids" who were helping him get the site ready during the summer. It was like "cleaning the Augean stables," she said, given all the old, caked grease. (I interviewed her for a 2019 *Cincinnati* magazine story, from which this chapter has been expanded.) But no matter—this was a mission. She was trying to help remake Cincinnati, to help it keep up with the boomer youth revolution. "It was a time when so much was going on everywhere," Winters said. "And we wanted a scene

Jim Tarbell (*left*) and Jim Knippenberg (*right*) on tall chairs at Ludlow Garage. *Photograph by Gary Becker; courtesy of the* Cincinnati Enquirer.

in Cincinnati, which felt like this backwater. And for a short time, Ludlow Garage was it."

While it lasted for just seventeen months, Ludlow Garage's existence disproved Winters's belief—shared by so many restless, coming-of-age Cincinnati teens and young adults at the time—that she lived in a cultural backwater. It was a primary stop on the national "ballroom" circuit that had grown up around the maturing of rock 'n' roll into progressive, evolving, experimental rock. Ludlow Garage was a worthy contemporary not just of the ballrooms in San Francisco, where the trend started, but also of such other big-city venues as the Boston Tea Party, the Fillmore East in New York City, Grande Ballroom in Detroit, the Family Dog in Denver, the Warehouse in New Orleans and the Agora Ballroom in Cleveland, among others.

If you're of a certain age and equate the city's cultural history with the concerts you've seen, then the brief but bright shining era of Tarbell's Ludlow Garage was Cincinnati's equivalent to Camelot. Its first headlining act, on September 19 and 20, 1969, was the then-super-hot Grand Funk Railroad (with Eli Radish as an opening act). It closed after one of its most legendary bookings—the avant-garde blues-jazz-rock visionary Captain Beefheart and Ry Cooder (with Pure Prairie League the listed opener) on January 19 and 20, 1971. In the *Independent Eye*, Cincinnati's bimonthly underground newspaper, a writer referred to Beefheart's Magic Band as "perhaps the weirdest looking people ever on a rock stage." That's saying something.

What happened in between captured the expansive changes that were occurring in rock and other popular music genres that appealed to the youth. The musicians had become increasingly ambitious and progressive in the wake of the Beatles, the Rolling Stones, Bob Dylan, the Band, Aretha Franklin and such Motown recording artists as Stevie Wonder, Marvin Gaye, the Supremes and many more.

Ray Davies brought his British band the Kinks to Ludlow Garage in 1969. *Photograph by Stu Levy.*

At the same time, rock had become the clarion call of a larger societal revolution that originated with the youth. The Garage represented those times and captured the zeitgeist as poignantly as any other local concert venue. It helped, of course, that it was an extraordinary time to be young.

Here's just a sample of the acts who came to the Garage at that time and are now considered among rock's most historically important (either creatively or commercially, or both) acts today: Bonzo Dog Doo Dah Band, the Holy Modal Rounders, the Kinks, the Incredible String Band, the Allman Brothers, the James Gang, Dr. John, the Night Tripper, NRBQ (frequent performers), Johnny Winter, Mountain, Fairport Convention and many more. For many acts, Ludlow Garage was their first Cincinnati booking. Others were able to use it as a stepping-stone and accelerate their rise to stardom. For instance, after the innovative new San Francisco Bay Area band Santana, headed by virtuosic guitarist Carlos Santana, played Xavier University's Schmidt Fieldhouse in support of headliner Arlo Guthrie and won raves, they hurried back to town less than two weeks later to headline for two nights at the Garage. It remains a favorite memory of those who patronized the Garage.

And Cincinnati's close connections to the fertile Michigan rock scene resulted in a lot of the Wolverine State's raucous, brash, musically and sartorially rebellious acts playing there. Aside from Grand Funk, there were the Frost, Iggy Pop's Stooges, MC5, the Sunday Funnies, the Amboy Dukes, Commander Cody and His Lost Planet Airmen, Alice Cooper (who had moved near Detroit from elsewhere) and the Bob Seger System. Cincinnati became a stronghold for Detroit rock.

Tarbell also included regional acts, like the Lemon Pipers, Whalefeathers, Balderdash, East Orange Express, Mad Lydia, Lonnie Mack and Sandy Nassan, on his bills, thus helping them. Looking at the list of such acts today is like doing a deep dig into Cincinnati and Ohio music history. Who exactly were Ed Chicken & the French Fries (an Antioch College band), and were they as good—or as bad—as their moniker?

While the Garage was hot, Tarbell sponsored a few shows at bigger venues—Neil Young, the Mothers of Invention, Herbie Mann and John Mayall at other Cincinnati locales and even a Badfinger show in Dayton. And also while the Garage was hot, it assembled a far-reaching ticket sales network: Kidd's Book Store, the Marlboro Book Store, the New York Times Clothing Store, Unique Basket Shops, Points East and other outlets in Dayton, Yellow Springs, Oxford and Athens, as well as in Louisville and Lexington, Kentucky.

Tarbell had a very expansive, eclectic enthusiasm for all music. And he took chances; he was willing to defy both conventional commercial wisdom and the city's default position: conservatism. When a somewhat-faded British Invasion group like the Kinks was ready to reconquer America with their new album, *Arthur*, Tarbell eagerly booked them.

The Garage also presented important soul, jazz, gospel and blues acts, like B.B. King, Bo Diddley, the Staple Singers, Roland Kirk and Tony Williams Lifetime, thus championing diversity. And that approach resulted in some thought-provoking moments, like when Roebuck "Pops" Staples, the Staple Singers' patriarch, introduced the hauntingly somber blues song "Battle of Birmingham" to the audience: "A few years ago, down in Birmingham, Alabama, a little girl wanted to go out and march, and her mother told her she was afraid for her to go out and march. She'd rather she go to church. And she went to church, and the church was bombed, and she was killed." (The show also featured Pops's young daughter, Mavis, who, today, is acknowledged as one of America's great singers, performing a searing, empowering version of the Band's "The Weight.")

Tarbell, now one of the city's civic elders (he's even the subject of an Over-the-Rhine tribute mural), remembered his motivation for opening Ludlow Garage, over the years repeating this viewpoint: "I also sensed that things were a bit confusing. Kids weren't communicating so well with their parents. They needed a place or places where they could compare notes on life, and that needed to be in the urban city. I was all about focal points."

Considering how fondly Ludlow Garage is remembered today, it's surprising to learn how hard it was to ever get it open. But then, considering how much of the emerging youth culture scared adults of the day—sex, drugs, rock 'n' roll, long hair and all that—maybe that should have been expected.

Tarbell originally wanted to locate the Garage in Clifton's Gaslight District to avoid the area around University of Cincinnati, where bars along Calhoun and McMillan Streets mixed party rock with alcohol. Tarbell didn't want that, as he felt it would limit teen attendance and encourage disrespectful listening. "I didn't like Calhoun Street," he said. "To me, it had run its course. It was kind of seedy. So, I purposely skipped over campus and was looking over Ludlow Avenue. And there was this building." (The Black Dome, an earlier attempt at a club featuring national progressive rock acts, had been located near UC.)

Ironically, after the Ludlow Garage's automotive business closed in 1966, the building was purchased by one of those very Calhoun Street venues, the Varsity Mug Club. Tarbell said it was eyeing the spot for an "inexpensive steak and beer" establishment. But the Clifton Town Meeting neighborhood association opposed its liquor license request. So, Tarbell was able to lease the space for about $400 a month. For the renovation, he raised roughly $75,000 from two key sources, whose children had been active with the Hyde Park Teen Center—primarily Robert D. Stern, of the family who founded U.S. Shoe, and J. Robert Orton Jr., the fourth generation of his family to own Railway Supply and Manufacturing Company and a visual arts patron who wrote a fascinating book about his passion, *Benevolence & Blasphemy: The Memoirs of a Contemporary Collector.*

While Tarbell and his crews started in on the renovation, he experimented with a couple of outside concerts. One, which is still a personal favorite of his, involved bringing in the Edwin Hawkins Singers, a gospel group that had an unexpected smash hit in 1969 with the euphoric "Oh Happy Day," to the Cincinnati Zoo's Whiting Grove Picnic Area in July 1969. (Sound Museum, a stylishly hip local jazz group featuring tenor saxophonist Jimmy McGary, opened.) "It was to preview the Garage," Tarbell explained. "We hid the choir in the woods, and they came out at twilight, holding candles and singing 'Joy! Joy!' I'm here to tell you, it doesn't get any better than that. It was one of those moments."

With the Ludlow Garage's scheduled opening just weeks away, on September 6, Tarbell brought the city's first fair-sized outdoor rock

This photograph, taken in 1981, gives an overview of Ludlow Garage's street presence. *Courtesy of the* Cincinnati Enquirer.

festival—the Midwest Mini-Pop Festival—to the zoo. It occurred three weeks after the Woodstock Festival in New York and even used some of Woodstock's sound system, which was shipped to Cincinnati for the Ludlow Garage. Tarbell had scheduled one of Woodstock's performers: the Paul Butterfield Blues Band, featuring Howard "Buzzy" Feiten on lead guitar and the now-deceased Butterfield on blues harp and vocals. And it even shared some of Woodstock's legendary torrential downpour, which resulted in a rain delay and people playing/sliding on a muddy hillside near the zoo's amphitheater.

But there were a few differences. Because it was held at a zoo rather than Yasgur's farm—in a locale near Forest Avenue, then known as the old Bear Pits area—concertgoers could hear the occasional caged animal roar. It was just one night, a Saturday, and drew as many as eight thousand people, modest by Woodstock standards. Aside from Butterfield, the biggest names were Vanilla Fudge and Grand Funk Railroad, popular in their time but not of enduring Woodstock superstar stature.

Three Cincinnati acts were to serve as openers, but according to a review in the *Independent Eye*, only a local rock quartet, Balderdash, which featured a dynamic organist in the late Steve Brady, played because of the rain delay.

"It was as close as most of that crowd got to Woodstock," said David Little, a Clifton resident and political consultant who attended the event as a music-loving teenager. He bought a five-dollar ticket at the gate.

Even after Tarbell proved he could stage a sizeable rock concert, factions in Clifton and city officials still fought him on numerous fronts over the Garage, although since he never wanted a liquor license, that wasn't an issue. He credits his powerful lawyer, S. Arthur Spiegel (subsequently a federal judge), for helping navigate the opposition.

"The first concert was scheduled to be at Ludlow Garage, with the Youngbloods [a group whose then-current hit was, fittingly, called 'Get Together'], Lonnie Mack and Balderdash," Tarbell recalled. "I came to the Garage one day, and there was a red sticker on my door that said, 'Stop work.' They [the city] made me put in a $25,000 extra exit out of the club. That wouldn't have happened if not for political pressure." On short notice, that opening show was transferred to the Emery Theatre in Over-the-Rhine. But by the next week, the Garage was open.

The still-striking photograph collage poster for that Grand Funk show—the first at the Garage itself—announced the new venue in an artful, avant-garde way that underscored the cultural radicalism inherent in the Garage's concept. Designed by the graphic arts firm Sontag, Bottoni and Levy, it featured a naked man, backside to the viewer and hands extended upward, standing between two giant earlobes. Combined, the images look like a butterfly and signaled that a transformation, a metamorphosis, was occurring.

After the Garage opened, community concern slowly subsided, more or less. There was a meeting in October 1969, where Tarbell told those disgruntled by the presence of the young people at his shows that the Garage was "a place to solve problems rather than create them." A June 1970 *Clifton Town Meeting* newsletter contained a "live and let live" column from its president, Harry M. Hoffheimer, which read, in part: "After failing in attempts to dissuade the management of the Ludlow Garage from opening a rock music hall at its present location, we nevertheless strenuously and successfully counseled some individuals, who would have attempted to block its operation through litigation, to refrain from that course."

Still, noise complaints were common. Tarbell remembers, at one point, Detroit's fiery MC5 was on stage, prodding the crowd to get excited. "A police officer came to the front door with his hand in his holster and said, 'Put it down or I'll put a hole in the speaker.'"

The Garage had a distinct visual look once it debuted as a club; with ten thousand square feet on each of its two floors, it was an early example of what's come to be known as adaptive reuse. Tarbell kept the two interior auto ramps at the front entrance. One went down, below the concert area, to a ticket-taking station, concession area (with macrobiotic food), offices and a dressing room. From there, patrons took steps up to see shows on the main floor. When the night was over, people could leave through two opened oversized doors, walk down the upper ramp and go out.

To pay respect to the building's history as an auto garage, the bathrooms had a motor-oil motif—Quaker State for men and Pennzoil for women. Inside, people found the kind of round terrazzo sinks used in factories or old schools; patrons operated them via a foot bar that sprayed water in all directions, so multiple people could wash at once. Tarbell purchased those secondhand, again to pay tribute to the building's history, and they remain among the most fondly remembered elements today. (An *Independent Eye* story at the time of the Garage's opening reported that Tarbell had hopes of creating a community center on the lower level.)

The concert space was more psychedelic than post-industrial and could hold as many as 900 people, Tarbell said, though its official capacity was less. (Another source says the Garage could squeeze in 1,200.) There were some pyramid-shaped plywood pieces that could be used for seating and jute reproductions of Persian rugs on the floor. Tarbell's friends from a "hippy farm" factory provided translucent candles that hung from the Garage's beams; after they burned to a certain point, votives were put inside. There were also six oversized chairs and rockers designed by the owners of a Mount Adams head shop called the Blown Mind. "The highchairs and rockers were all about this *Alice in Wonderland* idea I had about trying to do things that took you out of your element, with or without taking LSD," Tarbell said. (Drug use was discouraged at the Garage, as was cigarette smoking, Tarbell said.)

Inside, the lightshow crew FlavorScope, the creative high school students who had first produced their visual accompaniments to live music at the Tarbell-run Hyde Park Teen Center, returned to Ludlow Garage. "Each performance was an improvisation intended to accompany the music," said Bill Westheimer, now a New Jersey–based photographer. "We were listening to live music and reacting to it instantaneously and constantly creating new imagery to be used. We had a pretty big library of slides and sixteen-millimeter film. A lot of it was just scrap film we drew on with magic markers and Indian ink, stuff like that."

As an emcee and all-around exuberant presence at the Garage, Tarbell—with his distinctive and enthusiastic manner—was not some faceless promoter. He was a dynamic part of the Garage action, an exuberant emcee whose warm, friendly voice introduced acts.

Terry Adams, a member of then-new band NRBQ (he still fronts a version of the group), which played the Garage multiple times, once told me: "That Ludlow Garage was unlike any other place we ever played. In the traditional sense, [bands] are far-out, and club owners are businessmen. I would say Jim Tarbell was farther out than any band that ever played there—except for us. He was as creative a free spirit as anybody I ever met, and that's why we felt so at ease there and played several times. They also had a great crew there that recorded that stuff. That Ludlow Garage is a special place." (In 2006, NRBQ released a wildly joyful live album, *Ludlow Garage 1970*, from concert tapes made by the Garage's sound crew.)

Another person with fond memories of Ludlow Garage is Alice Cooper, who, on a video disc released with 2009's *Ludlow Garage 40th Anniversary Tribute* CD, said his band first created "I'm Eighteen," the late 1970 breakthrough hit and precursor of punk rock, while at Ludlow Garage earlier that year. "We wrote [it] there late one night—it was just a jam," he said.

There were also acts that were underappreciated at the time—or still—that deserved much better, such as Martha Veléz. On December 5, 6 and 9, 1969, Veléz played what was touted in the press as a debut performance. She brought along a band that included four alumni of Paul Butterfield's groups, including alto saxophonist David Sanborn. A New York native of Puerto Rican descent who had been in the London production of *Hair*, Veléz had released her first solo album, the bluesy, rocking *Fiends and Angels*, that included backup work from Eric Clapton, Christine McVie, Brian Auger and Jack Bruce. (Veléz later went on to collaborate with Bob Marley.) An *Independent Eye* review at the time said that the turnout was poor but Veléz was superb. You can hear what you probably missed by listening to the *Ludlow Garage 40th Anniversary Tribute* CD to her ripping interpretation of the early 1960s soulful hit "You're No Good," five years before Linda Ronstadt revived the song to far greater success.

You could fill a book with anecdotes about the quirks and unusualness of individual performers. Tarbell recalled, for instance, how Winged Eel Fingerling (Elliot Ingber), the guitarist with Captain Beefheart's Magic Band, "lived on a diet of nothing but oranges for a year, and I swear as we speak that his skin was orange."

Not all the national acts were as altruistic and utopian as the Garage's vibe and the times seemed to encourage. "The worst experience we had was opening for Grand Funk Railroad," said the now-deceased Bob Nave,

DO IT! AT THE LUDLOW GARAGE

PHIL OCHS

AND

JERRY RUBIN

Sunday May 10, 1970····· 7:30 p.m.

ALL PROCEEDS
FOR THE BENEFIT OF
·CHICAGO 10
·PANTHER 21
·G.I.CIVIL LIBERTIES
DEFENSE COMMITTEE

donation

$3

SPONSORED BY
CINCINNATI VETERANS FOR PEACE

A handbill for the show with radical Jerry Rubin and folk singer Phil Ochs. *Courtesy of Bill Soudrette.*

the keyboardist for the Lemon Pipers, an Oxford, Ohio–originated band that had a national hit in 1968 with "Green Tambourine." "They didn't want to share the dressing room with us. That was not a fun night." (The two groups shared a bill in February 1970.)

Tarbell let the Garage be used for political fundraisers and raising community consciousness. On May 10, 1970—a Sunday night just six days after the Ohio National Guard shockingly killed four students at Kent State University—some one thousand people (an estimate from *Independent Eye*) came to hear the radical firebrand (and native Cincinnatian) Jerry Rubin exhort them with his incendiary, sometimes hyperbolic, talk of worldwide anticolonialist, anticapitalist leftist revolution. Referring to the 1969 moon landing by U.S. astronauts, Rubin indignantly said, "They put an American flag on the moon! I swear that if I die doing it, I'm going to go up there and rip that flag down. The American flag has no business on the moon." Addressing places closer to home, Rubin said, "We've got to close down the schools. We've got to make sure they never open again, because schools are prisons. Close down UC. Close down Walnut Hills High School." (Rubin was a graduate of both.)

Tarbell has consistently spoken fondly of most of the acts that appeared at his ballroom, but he makes an exception for Rubin, whom he remembers telling his audience to "kill your parents." Rubin was infamous for coining that attention-getting term. "That was more than I bargained for," said a still-annoyed Tarbell.

At that same event, which also featured speakers and musical acts, the great Phil Ochs—probably rivaled in songwriting talent by only Bob Dylan among those musicians who emerged from the Greenwich Village folk movement of the early 1960s—performed a song adapted from Edgar Allan Poe's poem "The Bells," plus two of his own masterworks, "Pleasures of the Harbor" and "Changes."

In mid-1970, business at the Garage started to slow down. There was an article in the *Independent Eye* about Tarbell's financial troubles, although he remained optimistic. And by June of that year, the paper's listings column, "The Organized Effort," was noting that "the Ludlow Garage will be open at irregular times" and to call ahead. One reason for these problems was that the best of the new generation of rock acts had become so big so fast that they were then capable of playing much larger venues, and there was increased competition to book them. In the spring of 1970, the Who were at Music Hall, the Grateful Dead were at the University of Cincinnati's Armory Fieldhouse and ambitious pop festivals were produced at both Cincinnati Gardens and Crosley Field. (See chapter 13.) And there was also new club competition—a place called Reflections opened near UC in November 1970 with the James Gang.

Tracy Nelson, the lead singer of Mother Earth, a talented Tennessee-based blues and country rock band, remembers problems with the last of several gigs the band played at the Garage in May 1970. (At a gig in 1969, Boz Scaggs had played with Mother Earth as a guest.) "What I particularly remember was the last time we played there, he [Tarbell] was pretty much going out of business," she said. "At the end of the show, he just couldn't pay us. So, we took everything we could find that we wanted out of the dressing room in lieu of pay. I remember there were a couple Oriental rugs that I had for a very long time."

About the decline, Tarbell said he was losing interest as rock became a big business. "It was baptism by fire to realize how quickly the whole scene changed from peace and love to money."

Still, there were great shows throughout the rest of 1970. Captain Beefheart's first of two appearances at Ludlow Garage came on November 20 and 21, 1970, in a wild show that also paraded forth such colorfully named acts as Hampton Grease Band, Screaming Gypsy Bandits, Avenue of Happiness and Balderdash.

The Bloomington, Indiana–based Gypsy Bandits, which pushed jazz and progressive rock into a complex and exciting avant-garde fusion, included drummer Mike Bourne, a noted jazz scholar and theater critic who was already contributing articles to *Downbeat* when his band came to Cincinnati to play with Captain Beefheart (California native Don Van Vliet, who died in 2010). So, Bourne—a great admirer of Beefheart's music—interviewed him at the time for *DownBeat* and also wrote an insightful, learned review of the show. Of the Hampton Grease Band, whose leader was Colonel Bruce Hampton, Bourne praised his vocals and guitar work but worried about the opening-night volume. "I was, for the first time, truly conscious of the potential physical damage of high volume, so painful was the PA power," he wrote. (The superb Bourne Beefheart interview is available in the 2009 book *DownBeat: The Great Jazz Interviews: A 75th Anniversary Anthology*.)

By the way, the late Hampton's work is increasingly hailed today for its innovation. In his 2004 book, *Dixie Lullaby: A Story of Music, Race and New Beginnings in a New South*, Mark Kemp praises Hampton Grease Band as "the South's answer to Captain Beefheart, Frank Zappa and the Grateful Dead—combined."

The end for Ludlow Garage came with another Beefheart visit on January 19 and 20, 1971. Someone in the crowd filmed part of it (and it's available on YouTube); it was sensational in a far-out, mind-blowing way. Beefheart wails and moans through the surreal lyrics of "When Big Joan Sets Up" from his milestone *Trout Mask Replica*, while the urgently pulsating and exciting music, always flirting with cacophony, builds as the saxophone's otherworldly squeals seem to push up against the Garage's ceiling and the marimba tones shoot around the room like hail against a windowpane.

In Beefheart's Magic Band in 1971 was percussionist Art Tripp, also known as Ed Marimba, who had earlier attended the University of Cincinnati College-Conservatory of Music and even played with the Cincinnati Symphony Orchestra before moving away. "I was sorry to hear about Ludlow's closing, because it was a great venue, and local jazz/rock fans were big supporters of it," he said via email. "But all good things come to an end. At least, I'm pretty sure that they do."

Cincinnati Enquirer reporter Peter Kakel found the show a fitting ending to the Ludlow Garage—and to a golden era of Cincinnati concert venues: "Captain Beefheart and His Magic Band are an appropriate group for the final show at the Garage," he wrote. "Their musical freedom complements the free atmosphere which prevailed at the Garage. Ludlow Garage had a sense of community, which many of the other clubs in the area lack. It will be sorely missed by Cincinnati rock fans."

Many clubs featuring national rock acts have come and gone since the Garage closed in January 1971. A current club that has no business connection with Tarbell but is called Ludlow Garage opened in the 2010s on the lower level of that very same building.

But Tarbell's Ludlow Garage remains special, nonetheless. (It was certainly a stepping-stone for him, as he went on to start Arnold's Bar and Grill, be a champion of the Over-the-Rhine revival, and become politically active.) You can hear Garage music in recordings; besides NRBQ, the Allman Brothers Band released a highly praised album, *Live at Ludlow Garage 1970*, in 1990 that contains a forty-four-minute performance of "Mountain Jam,"

After Ludlow Garage, Jim Tarbell—seen here in 1981—went on to champion Over-the-Rhine and downtown. *Photograph by Mark Treitel; courtesy of the* Cincinnati Enquirer.

their chimeric transformation of Donovan's "There Is a Mountain" into an epic display of their dual-lead-guitar prowess, as well as Gregg Allman's keyboard work and singing.

There's also the active collectors circle devoted to acquiring Ludlow Garage concert posters, handbills, newspaper articles and advertisements. Bill Soudrette has amassed an amazing amount of Ludlow Garage (and other music) material—from the colorful posters for shows by Spirit, Ricky Nelson/Sons of Champlin to smaller but distinctive flyers featuring band names inside a Persian rug–styled decorative border. He picked up some of those flyers as a Garage patron fifty years ago. Their appeal hasn't aged when he shares them with others. "That's one thing just about everybody relates to—the bands you saw in your adolescence," Soudrette said. "People just light up—'I went to that show,'" he explained. Or they wish they had.

13

1970 CINCINNATI SUMMER POP FESTIVAL

*C*rosley Field in the West End, where the Cincinnati Reds played baseball from 1912 to June 24, 1970, was one of five sports palaces that debuted during what architecture critic Paul Goldberger has called "the first golden age of ballpark design." Replacing the earlier generation of wooden structures, where team owners had to worry about fires, with steel and concrete, such edifices created a sanctuary inside their street-facing brick walls. Fans in comfortable grandstand seats or sunny bleachers could relax and watch the often-leisurely game be played out on the green infield and outfield—simultaneously a part of the surrounding city and away from it. It's no wonder these places either had "field" or "park" in their names: Crosley Field, Ebbets Field, Wrigley Field and Fenway Park. (There was one outlier: Detroit's Tiger Stadium.)

Basically, Crosley Field was reserved for Reds baseball games. But there were some entertainment events for which the open field came in handy. In 1948, a Roy Rogers Rodeo took place there. The Beatles played there during their 1966 U.S. tour—their second Cincinnati appearance and one of their last public concerts as a band (see the separate chapter on the Beatles' shows at Cincinnati Gardens and Crosley Field, both now lost venues.) Also, the Ohio Valley Jazz Festival was located at Crosley from 1964 to 1970, after it began in 1962 at the Carthage Fairgrounds (now the Hamilton County Fairgrounds). The festival's roots were in the 1958 French Lick (Indiana) Jazz Festival, started by Newport (Rhode Island) Jazz Festival founder George Wein with Cincinnati concert promoter and publicist Dino Santangelo.

Iggy Pop's famous pose from the 1970s Summer Pop Festival at Crosley Field. *From www. iStock.com/Tom Copi.*

And then there was the Cincinnati Summer Pop Festival of June 13, 1970. It has had a continuing outsized impact on greater popular culture, courtesy of the then-twenty-three-year-old performer Iggy Pop, the charismatic and daringly physical front man of the Stooges, a defiantly loud and harsh Detroit band.

You may well have seen the photograph from his set; it's not an overstatement to call it iconic. Iggy Pop (born James Newell Osterberg Jr.) created rock 'n' roll mythology at the Cincinnati event. You can marvel at his sense of confidence and defiance that is visible during the song "TV Eye" in the way he stands—bare-chested, dog-collar-wearing, lean and possessed—amid the outreaching hands of his fans on the ballfield, in front of the stage. They are lifting him up—literally and metaphorically—and he is reaching out with a finger on his outward-pointing, gloved right hand.

He rules his world, which, at the moment that photograph was taken, is the crowd who came to Crosley Field on a Saturday to see twelve hours' worth of sets by the likes of Traffic, Grand Funk Railroad, Mountain, Alice Cooper, the Bob Seger System, Mott the Hoople, Ten Years After, Zephyr, Savage Grace, Damnation of Adam Blessing, Brownsville Station, Bloodrock, Third Power, Mighty Quick, Cradle and Sky—as well as the

Stooges. At least, we think that was the lineup—not everyone announced seems to have played, according to some accounts.

That almost-supernatural walk was not the only high point of Iggy Pop's breathtaking performance. Because a ninety-minute television program, condensed from the rockfest, called *Midsummer Rock* is available on YouTube, you can see the Stooges doing "TV Eye" and "1970"—the latter also featured the liberating, avant-garde free jazz saxophone work of Steve Mackay.

During one of Iggy Pop's repeated forays into the crowd from the stage, a fan provided him with a jar of peanut butter, which he smeared on his chest and then casually tossed chunks to those surrounding him. He'd use anything as an improvised prop in the throes of the frenzied pre-punk rock 'n' roll squall that his bandmates played. That, in a (pea)nutshell, has become his legend—raw power, indeed. And he has remained an active and primal music figure since 1970, despite some rough times. In 2010, the Stooges—Iggy Pop, James Williamson, Dave Alexander and Scott and Ron Asheton—were inducted into the Rock & Roll Hall of Fame. It helped that Iggy Pop, both as a Stooge and later, became quite a songwriter, writing or cowriting classics like "I Wanna Be Your Dog," "Search and Destroy," "The Passenger," "Five Foot One" and "Candy."

Not to be outdone on television, a twenty-two-year-old Alice Cooper (born Vincent Furnier), pre-stardom, also gave an unforgettable performance for *Midsummer Rock*, and like Iggy Pop, he seized an opportunity offered him by a fan. He and his band, also named Alice Cooper, put on a kind of happening—as much performance art as rock—onstage, accompanied by their song "Black Juju," with its spacey, eerie music reminiscent of early Pink Floyd. Cooper was wearing a kind of cape on his bare back, but it's split open so he could clutch it and pull it forward, over his chest. With a necklace that looked like a giant bracelet, mascara-darkened eyes and tight, glittery bellbottoms hanging precariously low on his hips, Cooper was a highly provocative stage presence. After several minutes of the band's ebbing and flowing music, he crouched in a knees-out position and started swinging a pocket watch in front of his tightly packed, curious audience. He intoned, like a hypnotist, "Bodies need rest." Suddenly, a hurled cake (a pineapple upside-down cake, according to www.dangerousminds.net) smashed into his face, near his mouth. He took a few seconds to let what happened sink in and then continued his performance, even sampling his just desserts.

The set ended with him placing sheets over stage equipment, band members, the audience and even himself. He left to applause—it was a killer set. Still haunting us today is the question, as someone on Pinterest asked: "Who brings a cake to a rock festival?" (The answer may be that it was brought because this was an all-day festival where folks were encouraged by promotional material to "bring blankets, pillows, watermelon, incense, ozone rice [*sic*], your old lady, babies, and other assorted goodies and do your own thing.")

Cooper would go on to develop a following as a shock act with a countercultural vaudevillian reputation, and he became more popular—but not as strangely arty—after his Cincinnati Summer Pop Festival show. And his band, by 1972, had learned to make catchier rock songs about teenage life that he could sing with verve, like "I'm Eighteen" and "School's Out." In 2011, the band Alice Cooper—including Cooper, Dennis Dunaway, Glen Buxton, Michael Bruce and Neal Smith—was inducted into the Rock & Roll Hall of Fame.

The television program *Midsummer Rock* also offered straightforward guitar rock from the highly energized Grand Funk Railroad and Mountain bands and a pleasingly melodic headlining set from the recently reformed British band Traffic, featuring confident twenty-two-year-old Stevie Winwood, who had already been a star for several years. He sang a lovely version of the British folk ballad "John Barleycorn," which was featured on the upcoming best-selling Traffic album *John Barleycorn Must Die*. Traffic entered the Rock & Roll Hall of Fame in 2004.

Quite a few of the Summer Pop Festival's acts, besides the Stooges, Alice Cooper and Grand Funk Railroad, had Michigan connections. The event's promoters, Michael Quatro and Russ Gibb, were from Michigan, and Cincinnati was a reasonably close destination for kids from Detroit, which had a huge, voracious music scene that liked loud, hard rock with an edge.

According to a document obtained by Cincinnati collector Bill Soudrette, the concert was produced by Gibb, Gabriel Glantz and Robert Bageris. They deposited a total of $35,000 at Manufacturer's National Bank of Detroit to start, and they each had a 27.16 percent interest in the venture. Quatro owned 18.52 percent. Cincinnati's A. Jaye Agency, which had been founded by Stan Hertzman in 1967 and booked local rock bands, worked with Quatro and Gibb. On March 26, the same parties had cooperated on the multi-act Cincinnati Pop Festival at Cincinnati Gardens, which was marred by a no-show from headliner Joe Cocker.

Top: A couple dances happily at Summer Pop Festival. *Photograph by Mark Treitel; courtesy of the* Cincinnati Enquirer.

Bottom: A hirsute man holds his hands out near police. *Photograph by Mark Treitel; courtesy of the* Cincinnati Enquirer.

Top: Festival crowd in stands. *Photograph by Mark Treitel; courtesy of the* Cincinnati Enquirer.

Middle: Grand Funk guitarist Mark Farner excites the crowd. *Photograph by Mark Treitel; courtesy of the* Cincinnati Enquirer.

Bottom: Police watch a couple perched on billboard. *Photograph by Mark Treitel; courtesy of the* Cincinnati Enquirer.

Above: A man standing in the grandstand. *Photograph by Mark Treitel; courtesy of the* Cincinnati Enquirer.

Left: A woman with a young child on her shoulders. *Photograph by Mark Treitel; courtesy of the* Cincinnati Enquirer.

The crowd passes a sprawled-out person on the sidewalk at Summer Pop Festival. *Photograph by Mark Treitel; courtesy of the* Cincinnati Enquirer.

Overall, as an event, the Cincinnati Summer Pop Festival has a checkered legacy. *Billboard*, the magazine of the music industry, reported in its July 4, 1970 issue, "Rock Fest in Cincinnati is $$ Success, but Rocked by Melee." Some 28,000 attended the event at $6.50 per person—Crosley's capacity for baseball was about 30,000—and there were 110 police officers on duty, paid for by Quatro. As chronicled in a 2010 *Cincinnati CityBeat* story, "A Summer to Remember," by Brian Powers, a public librarian who researched the festival for a fortieth anniversary presentation, the placing of the stage at second base created problems. The Reds, who still had several home games left, wanted police to keep people off the grass inside the baselines. The kids wanted to jubilantly dance. So, the setting wasn't relaxed. Press coverage at the time reveals that there was violence, with arrests involving mostly out-of-town youths after the event ended at midnight, and resultant charges of police brutality.

The *Midsummer Rock* TV broadcast, now an important and fascinating cultural artifact, was a product of Cincinnati television station WLWT (Channel 5), part of the Avco Broadcasting Corporation chain, and it was syndicated to stations across the country in August 1970. In most cities that broadcasted it, including Cincinnati, the audio was simulcast in stereo by FM rock stations. That broadcast has acquired a cult following. One source of the fascination was its host in the ballpark's broadcast booth: a straitlaced, coat-and-tie-wearing former *Today Show* announcer named Jack Lescoulie, who was hired for the occasion. (He was then fifty-eight and is now deceased.) Well-meaning but way out of his element, he comes off a bit like Fred Willard's announcer character in *Best in Show*. "That's peanut butter," Lescoulie exclaimed when Pop smeared the suspect substance on himself. Another time, the host complained that the bands did "not go about this in a showbiz way" because they spent too much time tuning up. "And kids don't seem to mind this at all." A younger WLWT employee, Bob Waller, provided colorful commentary and interviewed fans during the broadcast.

Oddly enough, when the Summer Pop Festival first was announced, via an advertisement in Cincinnati's bimonthly underground newspaper the *Independent Eye*, Three Dog Night was listed as the headliner. (The band, featuring three strong vocalists, was very successful at the time, although it was more of a top 40 act than a progressive rock band like the eventual top-of-the-bill choice, Traffic.)

Midsummer Rock's director was Bob Heath, who worked on WLWT's *Midwestern Hayride* and *50-50 Club*, and he was brought into the project by Bill Spiegel, also a *Hayride* veteran. WLWT had been broadcasting Reds games at Crosley Field for years, so it was familiar ground for the camera and sound crew.

In a 2010 interview with me for *Cincinnati CityBeat*, Heath explained that Avco wanted to tap into the counterculture after Woodstock the previous summer showed how big it was. So, when a mystery man out of New York named Michael Goldstein pitched a broadcast of the Cincinnati Pop Festival, Avco told him to do it. Spiegel and Heath were willing, but the rest of the station management was reluctant. "Spiegel was great, but the people above him said, 'We've got to protect ourselves,'" Heath recalled. "So, they brought in Jack Lescoulie and said, 'This will sanitize it for sponsors and the audience in Cincinnati.' Lescoulie was a very nice man, but [he] didn't belong at a Rock concert."

While Heath's crew—with three cameras at their disposal—taped everything, they had to select just five acts for the ninety-minute broadcast. Grand Funk and Traffic were picked because they opened and closed the event, and Mountain was chosen because the Cream-influenced group was a favorite of producer Goldstein's. Heath can't remember why Alice Cooper—whose music was unmelodic and semi-experimental—was chosen, although the cake incident might have played a role. But of the choice of the Stooges, there was never any doubt. The crew knew immediately when a great moment in rock had occurred. "We chose Iggy because of the visuals of him with the peanut butter and standing in the crowd," Heath said. "All the other groups were rock and rollers who performed in a 'glass wall' way: 'I'm on stage, you're in the audience.' [Iggy] made it theater—pure entertainment as opposed to just being music-based. Now, look at all the groups that do that."

After the Reds left Crosley Field, the Ohio Valley Jazz Festival's final stand at the ballpark occurred on August 15, 1970, with the Kenny Burrell Quartet, Gene Ammons and Sonny Stitt, Roberta Flack, the Eddie Harris Quartet, the Cannonball Adderley Quartet, the Les McCann Quartet and the Herbie Mann Quintet.

And then, on September 19, with little advance notice, Isaac Hayes— who was then enjoying massive success as a low-voiced romantic crooner known as "Mr. Hot Buttered Soul"—showed up with opening acts Cincinnati Joe, the Bar-Kays and Luther Ingram. The *Enquirer*'s Jim Knippenberg attended the show and reported the crowd was "relatively small but very vocal." And the end of his review served as a fitting end to Crosley Field: "It was Hayes they all came to see, and it was Hayes who they smothered in affection. It was also Hayes who made the night one to remember for a while."

After the city acquired the site from the Reds, it used it as an auto impound lot while planning future development. The demolition began on April 19, 1972.

Crosley Field is now lost but is still dearly missed by fans of both Cincinnati baseball and Iggy Pop.

SELECTED INDEX

A

Albee Theatre 70
Alibi Club 24
Apartment 67, 68
Armory Fieldhouse, University of
    Cincinnati 157
Arnold's Bar and Grill 11, 158
Aunt Maudie's 91

B

Babe Baker's Jazz Corner 13, 101,
    103, 104
Baby Grand 91
Barn and the Hangar 67
Beatles concerts in Cincinnati 18,
    32, 39, 43, 44, 45, 47, 49, 51,
    60, 109, 110, 111, 112, 113,
    114, 118, 119, 120, 121, 127,
    142, 149, 161
Beverly Hills Country Club/Supper
    Club 21, 23, 30, 53, 61, 65

Black Dome 10, 133, 135, 136,
    138, 139, 140, 141, 142, 143,
    145, 146, 151
Blind Lemon 86, 145
Blue Angel 67, 68, 73
Bogart's 95
Buccaneer Inn 91

C

Cabana Lounge 91
Carousel Inn 91
Carthage Fairgrounds 161
Castle Farm 46, 59, 60, 89
Catacomb Hideaway 77
Cat & Fiddle 68
Cedar Bar 21
Cincinnati Gardens 13, 39, 40, 41,
    43, 45, 46, 109, 111, 112,
    114, 120, 145, 157, 161, 164
Cincinnati Summer Pop Festival
    (1970) 13, 157, 161, 162,
    164, 168

Cincinnati Zoo 11, 40, 151
Club Ramon 94
Club Touchez 34, 92
Club Tulu 34, 87
Cock & Bull 91
Copa Club 24, 27, 29, 105
Cotton Club 89, 91, 103

D

Danny's Jubilee Lounge 91
Downstairs Club 33
Dude Ranch 92
Duffy's Tavern 102

F

Family Owl at the Candlelight 96, 97
Fine Arts Plaza 93
Flamingo Club 29, 30, 34, 71

G

Gayety Burlesque 69
Glen Rendezvous 23
Golden Door 96
Golden Lounge 26
Gooch's Web 23
Guys and Dolls 34, 35, 36, 37

H

Herbie's Neoteric Jazz Lounge 91
Hustler Club 68
Hyde Park–Mount Lookout Teen
    Center 16, 125

I

Inner Circle 95, 96

J

Jazz Bohemia 90
Jockey Club 11, 34
Joe's Lake 21

K

Kasbah, Terrace Hilton 67
Ken Mill Tavern 84
Key Room 91
Kolping Grove 137

L

Lakeridge Hall 137, 146
Leo Coffeehouse 77
LeSourdsville Lake Amusement
    Park 92
Living Room 53, 65, 66, 67, 68,
    72, 73, 91
Lockland Roller Dome 91
Log Cabin 103
Lookout House 21
Love's Coffee House 96
Ludlow Garage 10, 11, 13, 14, 18,
    83, 87, 130, 133, 135, 145,
    147, 148, 149, 150, 151, 153,
    154, 155, 157, 158, 160

M

Misty Lounge 91
Moonlite Gardens, Coney Island
     36, 58
Mother's 23, 91
Music Hall 14, 16, 32, 40, 46, 47,
     60, 89, 157

N

Netherland Hilton 77
New Cotton Club 91
936 Club 91

O

Ohio Valley Jazz Festival 51, 68,
     101, 110, 161, 170

P

Panacea 145
Peebles Corner Nite Club 68
Penthouse 67, 68, 71
Piano Lounge 65, 66, 67, 71
Pickle Barrel 96, 136
Playboy Club 67, 69, 91
Playhouse in the Park 76
Prophet 83, 84, 86

R

Rainbow Club 91
Rathskeller, Sheraton-Gibson 68

Reflections 157
Regal Theater 93
Ritz Ballroom 91
Riverfront Coliseum 49
RKO Palace 70
Round Table 96

S

Schmidt Fieldhouse, Xavier
     University 51, 137
Seven Cities 9, 13, 75, 76, 77, 79,
     80, 81, 82, 83, 86, 87, 90
Shubert Theatre 65
Sign of the Drum 69
Spatz Show Bar 92
Sportsman's Club 23, 24, 26, 27
Stein's Hideaway 91
Surf Club 53, 54, 55, 56, 57, 58,
     59, 60, 61, 62, 63, 65, 90
Swifton Shopping Center 60, 93
Swing Bar 91

T

Taft Theatre 14
Tommy Helms's Dugout 71
Top Shelf 91
Trip 71
Twin Drive-In 93

V

Varsity Mug Club 87, 151
Vet's Inn 91

W

Wein Bar 97, 98, 99, 100
Western Woods Mall 93
Whiskey-A-Go-Go Discotheque 71
Whisper Room 91

Y

Yeatman's Cove, Sheraton-Gibson 69

ABOUT THE AUTHOR

Steven Rosen has worked for the *Cincinnati Enquirer*, *Denver Post*, *Cincinnati CityBeat* and other newspapers. Among his assignments, he served as the Arts & Culture editor at *Cincinnati CityBeat* and the art and film critic (and a music writer) at the *Denver Post*. As a freelancer, he has written for *Cincinnati Magazine*, *New York Times*, *Los Angeles Times*, *Boston Globe*, *American Songwriter*, *Documentary Magazine*, *IndieWire*, *Variety*, *Blurt*, *Rock & Roll Globe* and other outlets. He also founded National One Hit Wonder Day and started a music fanzine called *One Shot*. He is a member of the Cincinnati Vinyl Club and the Rock & Read Music Book Discussion Group. This is his first book.